Bolder and Wiser

C000277255

'This is a fascinating read. I've rare_
happen as I get older – I've been too focused on what the rest
of weeks might bring. But reading the perspectives of a range of older
women has really challenged me and provoked me to think harder.
A welcome experience!'

—Kathy Sykes, Professor of Sciences and Society, University of Bristol

'This book is funny, thought-provoking, inspiring and full of wisdom.
A timely read – I'm approaching 50 and the territory ahead has seemed
daunting and uncharted. However, I feel like I've been on a challenging,
but uplifting and nourishing, journey with a bunch of wonderful, wise
women, whose voices will remain with me.'

—Liz Hall, Author of *Mindful Coaching* and Editor of *Coaching at Work*

'Bolder and Wiser *made me laugh, but it also made me feel tingly with
emotion, even tearful, because I recognised so many of these women's
experiences – particularly their feelings about their appearance as
they aged.'*

—Justine, Sarah's hairdresser

'Grow (b)old along with me
The best is yet to be'

—John, Sarah's husband, with apologies to Robert Browning

About Sarah Dale

 Sarah is a practising occupational psychologist and accredited coach. She designed the structured coaching programme Creating Focus (**www.creatingfocus.org**) and is the author of *Keeping Your Spirits Up*, a guide to facing the challenges of modern life. She lives in Nottingham with her husband, two daughters and step-son. Her moments of leisure are spent Nordic walking, reading fiction and frequenting coffee shops, the more independent the better. She secretly loves a good jigsaw.

Bolder

AND

Wiser

REMARKABLE CONVERSATIONS
WITH OLDER WOMEN

SARAH DALE

Creating Focus Publishing

First published in 2013 by Creating Focus Publishing

www.creatingfocus.org

©Sarah Dale 2013

ISBN 978-0-9569169-2-1

Design and typesetting: Kate Ferrucci/Quarto Design, kate@quartodesign.com

Editorial consultancy: Lisa Hughes

Artwork: Judy Liebert, from a series on domesticity

For all generations of Bolder and Wiser women

For my daughters and my mum

For my twenty women

And in fond memory of Pam

CONTENTS

*No time to waste – deferred gratification – being a good old
person – retirement – invisible? – what matters – what doesn't*

*Shape-shifting – maintenance – hair – clothes – extreme
measures – perspective and dining tables – what matters –
what doesn't*

*Decisions, decisions – a sense of us – a sense of me –
negotiation – the long view – love, sex and romance –
what matters – what doesn't*

*Breaking out of perfectionism – the intrepid traveller –
making a difference – adventures in creativity – memories –
encouragement and equipment – what matters – what doesn't*

*The umbilical yank – an inexact science – independence and
identity – qué será será – all or nothing – what matters –
what doesn't*

*Worry and the unknown – sadness – making hay while the sun
shines – the shoebox – resilience – blessings – what matters –
what doesn't*

PREFACE

When I turned forty, I went to Cuba. It was a sponsored trek, raising money for the mental health charity, Mind. I didn't know anyone else who was going. Perhaps unsurprisingly, several other people had gone in milestone years. I fondly remember spending one evening with three other women: one turning thirty, one fifty and one, Pam, was just sixty. She had two grown daughters, and was a widow. I had two young daughters and was divorced. We didn't have a lot else in common. Our lifestyles and backgrounds were very different. We had grown up at opposite ends of the country. Our paths were unlikely to have crossed were it not for this trip. We got on like a house on fire.

Coming home, we met up two or three times over the following couple of years. Our lives didn't naturally overlap. I never met any of her family. So I was all the more saddened when her daughter rang me unexpectedly to tell me that Pam had died after a short but brutal illness. She was only 63.

I think my short friendship with Pam planted the seeds for this book. My time in Cuba was a strange bubble of intense experience, not connected with any other part of my life. I have not stayed in touch with anyone else from the trip. Without her, I don't share any memories of it with anyone. I wasn't in contact with home for the ten days I was there. The days were filled with strenuous walking, beautiful scenery, music and laughter as well as oddly deep conversation with strangers. Pam and I discussed everything that mattered to us: relationships, friends, independence, home, children, finance, curiosity, age and health. We howled with hysterical laughter like teenagers. We shared experiences which formed jewel-like memories for savouring later: the sunrise over the sea; startlingly bright star light; the sounds of a makeshift band floating across a hot and sunny farmyard; the taste of tropical fruit ripened on the tree.

Rolling forward a few years, with fifty lurking just beyond the horizon, I can feel the stirring of another stage of life. This isn't necessarily unpleasant although it is not exactly comfortable. It is a time of restlessness, curiosity, some shifting sands (and waistlines). I began to reflect that our lifestyles today don't always build in the opportunity to hear from women who have been there first. I spend a lot of time with my own generation, but not as much with others. My conversations with my mother and aunt are not quite the same as they are with other women of their generation. And I also realise how much I have benefited over the years from conversations with women (and men) half a generation ahead of me. They were not my parents and not my contemporaries. It gave them an interesting perspective.

I found I kept thinking about it. I set out to find twenty women, all at least ten years older than me, who were willing to chat to me about what matters and what doesn't, as they look back.

A word about men

I like men. The women I interviewed like men. We all know wise, funny, kind and endlessly supportive men and value them immensely. There are times when male physical strength makes me feel both valued and safe: the offer of a steady or helping hand for instance. I rarely feel offended or patronised by such gestures, or by well-intentioned and polite acts of kindness such as holding a door open or offering me a seat.

I struggle with the word *feminism* because of the connotations it can have. Despite my best efforts, word association still brings terms like 'strident', 'bra-burning', 'anti-men' and 'extremist' to my mind. But equality is extremely important to me. Some struggles for equality have been forceful or violent and from what I can tell, needed (and perhaps still need) to be. Some women have demonstrated extraordinary courage in standing up for all of us. Winning equal voting rights was shockingly hard work. So is winning equal educational, health and economic rights for girls and women around the world. These fights can be bloody and are far from over in many arenas.

My experience has been blessed by comparison. My expectations and opportunities for education were equal to my brother's. I have had many male colleagues and friends who have treated me as their equal. I have never felt owned or objectified and I have rarely felt overtly discriminated against.

I *have* had occasions where I have felt dismissed, ignored or over-ridden by virtue of my gender whether men (or women) intended to or not. I am well aware of systemic biases in many of our organisations and institutions, and threaded throughout our culture and society that keep inequality alive. Some are more subtle than others.

As I get older, I am increasingly aware that age adds another potential inequality to the mix. Being an older woman could hold a double whammy. Semantics aside, if feminism means believing in economic, social and political equality with men I am a feminist. Gender equality to me doesn't mean men versus women, or men and women being the same. Likewise, I don't expect (and wouldn't want) people in their sixties, seventies and beyond to be the same as those in their twenties – but I do believe in their economic, social and political equality. This book is my way of exploring what older women have to say, and helping me to work out what I think and feel about my own way forward.

It is difficult to separate out the ageing from the gender issues. No doubt some aspects of the conversations and what I've written apply equally to men. But I feel that women in particular are still in the early stages of developing acceptable or desirable models of ageing. This is a luxury previous generations of women didn't have. In the UK, women did not get equal voting rights until 1928, a year after the oldest of my interviewees was born. In addition, it was only two years before I was born that the contraceptive pill was made freely available in the UK. It wasn't until 1974 that the introduction of family planning clinics could begin to break down some of the taboos around single women and contraception.

In historical terms, these things alone have led to very recent and dramatic changes in what life might look like for women of any age. It is only now that women brought up with these changes are reaching older age. If I'd been interviewing the mothers and grandmothers of my group of women, almost all would be married, not employed outside of the home, subservient to their husbands (comfortably or not), unlikely to have been educated and probably a mother many times over. Their single or childless sisters would probably have been consigned to primary carer role for the extended family.

My grandparents were born early in the twentieth century. They were all, bar one, from large families. Their mothers' lives were taken over, or cut short by, the demands that this entailed.

They are shadowy figures in my understanding of our family tree. By the time they reached sixty, the women who were still alive would either have occupied the matriarchal role or have been quite simply worn out from hard work and life-long restriction. Of course healthcare advances have also changed the landscape of older age for men and women alike.

The whole concept of older women with energy, choice, education, and much closer to equal status with men is therefore relatively new, and still evolving. There isn't much of a road map. The generation I've been interviewing is at the cutting edge. It feels important to me to hear what they have to say about it.

Why *these* women?

These particular women were drawn to me, and me to them, by an informal process. Some are friends of my parents, some are parents of my friends, some were recommended via wider networks as inspiring women to speak to. I only knew four of them in any depth beforehand. One of those is my mother. They are not a sociologically representative sample. They are women whose life, experience or outlook resonated with me for some reason. I do not want to emulate any one of them as I grow older but there are aspects of each and every one that I admire or recognise or that I hope rub off on me.

One of the main things that they have turned out to have in common is that they are all curious about the world and themselves. They all value education highly and are life-long learners, both formally and informally. Many have professional qualifications too. For several, their formal higher education took place long after they left school. I was the first in my immediate family to go to university, as were many of the women I spoke to.

Curiosity clearly is not always about formal education either. Pam, who I introduced at the outset, had little formal education but her zest and curiosity for life were evident in everything I saw her do or heard her say.

None of the women live in poverty though the majority were born into modest circumstances. I would say that education, over one or two generations, has been the single biggest factor in changing those circumstances. The lifestyle they can afford now has been earned, by them and sometimes by also supporting their husbands' careers, rather than given to them.

In demographic terms, these women range in age from sixty to eighty-five. Three quarters of them were born and raised in the UK, the rest have started or continued life in India, New Zealand, USA, Germany, South Africa and the Netherlands. They cover the whole political spectrum. Sixteen of them have children. Nine are grandmothers. Fifteen of them currently live with a partner or husband. I wouldn't describe many of them as exactly retired. Some still do paid work, and some do voluntary work. They are all actively involved in their families and communities, and many of them are developing their creativity like never before.

There have been high points and low points. Between them, these women have received national honours and awards, raised hundreds of thousands of pounds for charity, published books, nurtured gardens, won elected office, been at the most junior and senior levels in their organisation, completed degrees at all stages of life, set up and run businesses, worked in factories, worked as cleaners, employed cleaners, supported others, raised children, cared for the sick and dying, challenged Government policy, held exhibitions and appeared on our national stage and television. They have had adventures and misadventures. They have dealt with major setbacks and disappointments. More than one is lucky to be alive now after serious accident or illness. Some have suffered heart-rending bereavements, and some have experienced significant moments of despair. All have cooked, cleaned and bottle washed to some extent at some time, some more than others. Some have travelled far, some stayed close to their roots.

This may make it sound like an unusual and remarkable group. It *is* remarkable. But I believe, from my experience as a psychologist and from observing women around me, that it may not be as unusual as it sounds. I suspect we would all be surprised by what we discovered if we took *any* group of twenty women over sixty and listened to them properly.

Whilst I hesitate to use the word ordinary, these women do not consider themselves to be anything unusual. I deliberately did not set out to find celebrities, even though some of them are well-known in their fields. I am not a celebrity. I wanted to listen to women who offered some resonance with my life. Of course, barely into most of these conversations, I quickly confirmed what I knew would be the case. Every story is unique and interesting. I was confident that would be the case at the outset and I wasn't disappointed.

These are the women we might stand next to in the queue for the ladies' toilet, or sit next to on the train. We see, but probably don't notice, them in supermarkets and cafes. In a busy and fragmented lifestyle, it is all too easy to overlook what they have to offer. Older women can be dismissed as eccentric, grumpy or quiet, or are only familiar in their relationships to other people – mother, grandmother, aunt, wife. We need to challenge our perceptions and our prejudices.

What this book is about

I have taken a very personal approach to this book. It is not a description of these women's lives and experiences. It is a book about my reaction to what I heard and how that is changing my own ideas and intentions about how I want to live my life from fifty onwards.

The whole project has been more therapeutic for me than I had expected though in hindsight I don't know why I am surprised by that. The support, challenge and inspiration I have gained from listening to these women's reflections has altered how I see myself and other women around me.

It has made me think hard about what I hope for me, my female friends, my daughters and their friends, and my mum. Interestingly, it has also made me think about what I hope for my husband, his son, my dad and my brother. I have especially begun to reflect on women's place and influence in the wider world, and the way men and women work and live together.

It has made me feel more accepting of the past, content with the present and more optimistic about what lies ahead. I'd love you to come along with me - we'll become bolder and wiser together!

INTRODUCING THE WOMEN

Each woman's story could form the basis of a book in itself. There is so much material I am reluctantly leaving out. The transcript of the conversations came to 155,000 words, based on around forty hours of interview.

After much thought and debate, I have decided to give a few details of each of the women, most of them under a pseudonym, and to focus on why I was drawn to them.

Twenty is too many to absorb at once, in the same way that it would be if we were introduced to twenty people at a party or a meeting. I don't expect you to read through all of these and remember them. Use this section as a reference point. You can return to it if and when you want to, as you read other chapters. The women are introduced in alphabetical order.

Throughout the book, italics will be used for quotes from the conversations themselves. The rest is my commentary.

This is not an academic text, but occasionally, I have referred to research. The references can be found at the end of the book. I also list some other books I read whilst I was working on this one.

As a life-long bookworm, I love to be given reading recommendations, so I also asked the women themselves to suggest one or two favourite books. These are listed alongside my background reading.

Anne

I was born in Glasgow in 1953, to a dad who was in the Royal Navy. We went all over the place. My most lovely time was between the ages of 9 and 10 in the Bahamas. But once you've left a place, that's it. You move on to the next one. And that's really been my style in life.

Why I was drawn to Anne

Anne was introduced to me by an old friend. She has been involved in politics and public service all her life, being married to an MP and – since our conversation – being elected as a County Councillor. She has a keen awareness of local and national issues and is on the boards of several organisations including a university, and a theatre and arts group.

She is animated and passionate, has a keen eye for the underdog – and is a good listener. Our conversation made me realise that women like Anne put themselves forward not because they are supremely confident or already know what they are doing, but because they are prepared to learn and want to make a difference. It isn't as easy as it may sometimes look from the outside.

She is a good example of someone who has made good use of opportunities as they have arisen and I reflected how that also isn't as easy as it sounds. Sometimes we bemoan our lack of opportunities whereas the truth may lie closer to being fearful of noticing or responding to them. Our own attitudes and personalities are important ingredients but so is support and encouragement from people around us. I was left with a lot of food for thought in terms of how this mix operates in my life. Interesting.

Her advice for younger women?

Do not worry about things you cannot know about. When I was 40 I was very worried about what life would be like when I was older. I have realised that the possibilities are numerous – both good and bad – and that I have a great deal of experience in making the best of difficult situations. So I have fewer expectations and more ambitions.

....

Cecelia

I was born in London in 1943. I was evacuated to Kent but I don't remember a thing about that. It is relevant I suppose that my mother died when I was three and my brother was one.

Why I was drawn to Cecelia

I have met Cecelia a few times socially as she is a friend of my parents. I find her bubbly interest in people and unguarded opinions refreshing and entertaining, and I guessed that our conversation was going to be a frank one. Her appreciation for people, ideas and design that she likes is heartfelt and I came away inspired to make more of an effort in the clothes department, as well as feeling that my parents have a very loyal friend in her.

She has suffered far more than her fair share of untimely bereavements, and I have to admit to feeling rather over-awed by this. I have been much more fortunate and have no idea how I would deal with what she has lived through. But what I did come away with was the knowledge that although these things cannot help but be life-changing, she has certainly not lost her joy in life. Bringing up two boys and being a very new grandmother has been a core part of her life. She is one of several of my interviewees who went to university in adulthood, with the support of her husband, where she studied art history and literature.

Her warm encouragement and support is readily shared and I came away fired up with enthusiasm for this project. She underestimates her own abilities and potential – as a woman she's not alone there – and our conversation reminded me just how important it is for us to support and encourage each other. Throughout her life, she has lost key relationships that would have provided some of that support. This makes her achievements all the more impressive.

Her advice for younger women?

Try and discover what your talents are and make the most of them. Don't let negative thoughts hold you back. Get a career. Just do the things you would like to explore and don't think you have all the time in the world to do them. Worship your body, feed it, exercise it, give it plenty of sleep, fresh air and look after it. Always moisturise your face! Do yoga, stay supple. Remember the maxim – don't interfere with nature and it won't interfere with you. Nurture your strength of spirit. Count your blessings. For me, I like having The Desiderata *to hand to ground me.*

....

Christine

I was born during the Berlin airlift. My parents lived in a little basement, in one room. My brother was three. Both families, before the war, were well to do. My mother was married when she was 17 to a second cousin and the marriage broke up but she was pregnant. He fathered another child. I think she had a traumatic time fleeing from East Prussia and being pregnant. My father was a student, two years younger than my mother – so he married a divorced woman who was pregnant. There were two more children after me. Eventually, we moved to West Germany because the wall came up. Our family was separated; some people lived in the East and some in the West.

Why I was drawn to Christine

Christine is sparky and no-nonsense, a great enthusiast. She's a mother of three grown up children, and a physiotherapist by occupation. I'd not met her before. She described herself as something of a tomboy when she was a child and painted a vivid picture of her childhood in post-war Berlin and Dusseldorf. She moved to the UK after the completion of her training as a physiotherapist and has lived here ever since.

In recent years, she has become involved in charities working with children and training therapists and carers in Eastern Europe and Africa. She deliberately tested her independence by travelling alone to these projects. She and her husband have travelled together at other times.

I warmed to her honest reflection on the highs and lows of parenthood and her sense of purpose about wanting to make a difference in her work. Her passion throughout her career has been working with children, families and schools – in both paid and voluntary roles. Her moving reflections on the impact of losing her mother at a relatively young age (she was 34, her mother 58) have stayed with me too. I left feeling keen to make the most of the relationships I have, whilst at the same time feeling that it was still possible to have some adventures and further your work too.

Her advice for younger women?

Go for it, it is truly never too late! Get out of your comfort zone every now and then and you will discover much, not least about yourself. Don't let anybody (yourself included) stop you from trying what you always wanted to explore or experience. If you are in a relationship, try and give each other space as well as enjoying new things together. Be yourself.

....

Helen

My parents had a business in Eastwood, DH Lawrence country. I was born in 1951, the same year as the Festival of Britain. Home was an adventurous, big, rambling place. My parents had a shop – three storeys plus attic, cellar, workshops, outbuildings – the perfect adventure playground. The adventurous spirit I developed so early has taken me around the world, through several careers and, now, having recently retired from twenty years of teaching in higher education, I work as a coach and Reiki practitioner as well as once again developing my creative practice.

Why I was drawn to Helen

I know Helen as we live in the same neighbourhood. I think of her as a colourful person – both with a very good eye for colour and textile in a literal sense, but also with a very lively and colourful way of telling stories and asking questions. She is one of life's great cheerleaders and despite having to learn to live with chronic illness, she maintains an enthusiasm for a wide range of people and ideas and always has something interesting to say.

As a child growing up with brothers, she describes herself as a tomboy and something of a wild child. Rebellious as a teenager and young adult, she had plenty of adventures before training in textile design. She excelled at this, becoming the director of a large textile company as well as going on to teach design history at university level. Since retiring from that on health grounds, she has trained as a life coach. She lives happily alone and has a real facility for living in and appreciating the present moment.

I am always energised by conversations with her, but this one even more so as I was able to hear her view on what matters and what doesn't. Her lack of materialistic ambitions, along with the way she has learnt to manage her condition, means that she focuses on the free or very inexpensive daily pleasures and joys that are there for all of us if we do but notice them. It is a refreshing lens through which to view the world.

Her advice for younger women?
Get fit and stay fit. Live every day as fully and as richly as you can. Help others along the way. Be kind to yourself.

....

Jane

I was born in Surrey in 1949, the third of four children. My father did a science degree, and then went into teaching, had a broken love affair and went out to Nigeria with the Methodist Mission Field. He came back in the war, with all the U-boats round him, and because he had ankylosis spondylitis [form of arthritis] wasn't allowed into the forces. He was scheduled

*to drive ambulances whilst he did his theology degree at
Cambridge – which is where he met my mother. My mother was
evacuated from Bedford University in London where she was
doing English and botany so she's actually got a London and
Cambridge degree.*

Why I was drawn to Jane

Jane first came to my attention via an event at Nottingham
University. A nurse by training, her career has taken her to the
highest levels of her profession, leading to national honours
and awards. She now works as an independent consultant, is a
keen champion of women and holds many advisory and board
positions. This could all have been somewhat intimidating, and
I can imagine that she can be pretty formidable when needs be.

However, her commitment and passion for the patients, staff
and students she ultimately cares for came through very clearly
indeed in our conversation. I was left with a deep appreciation
that women (and men) like her are prepared to dedicate their
lives to services that affect every one of us. Something feels right
in the world.

Our conversation also revealed a vulnerable side. Life has
thrown some significant setbacks her way. Not least of these is
not having children of her own, although she is a devoted aunt
and great-aunt. She has affected the lives of countless children
through her specialist work in children's health services. She and
her siblings are also dealing with the challenge of caring for their
mother. Both of these things are very levelling – her experiences
will be shared by thousands of women in all walks of life.

I came away from our conversation feeling humbled. Instead
of feeling intimidated by very successful women, we really do need
to cheer them on. They need it just as much as the rest of us do.

Her advice for younger women?

Take every opportunity as it presents itself – it may not come round again.

....

Jeannie

I was born during the war just outside London. There was a lot of activity. My father was stationed up in Scotland and my mother took me off to Ilfracombe to get away from the bombs. When I was five we moved to Worthing because my mother had always wanted to run a guest house. My father was a barber by trade but during the war had become a batman to an officer, so he was in a good position to be a waiter at the guest house.

Why I was drawn to Jeannie

Jeannie is an actor and presenter. I didn't know her but I can remember seeing her on schools television when I was at primary school. It was exciting to meet her. The anticipation built up by school's broadcasts in the seventies, when there was such a scramble to watch it as it was broadcast, would not be understood by today's children. She was also the voice on BBC Radio's *Listen with Mother*.

Her work has been much more than that however. A leading light in the actors' union, Equity, she has dedicated much of her time to campaigning for equality for women in the business. She was a key character in a long running British soap opera, and one of the founding members of the National Theatre. As a mother to a grown up son and daughter, she is tireless in working to bring about change for younger women wishing to work in television or acting *and* have a family, as well as working to change perceptions of, and opportunities for, older women in the media.

My conversation with her led me to reflect on some of the on-going inequalities for women to be heard in the wider world. With her beautifully clear speaking voice, she is articulate, expressive and downright angry about the inequalities that she has witnessed and experienced. I felt the call to action loud and clear. I hope that this book acts as something of a contribution.

Her advice to younger women?

Life is a learning curve and the more you know the more you realise how little you know and how much is left to learn. Have confidence in yourself and your value as a person. Be kind to your sisters. Don't be controlled into believing women are in competition with each other. Women have a great capacity for nurturing each other and often it is men who make us compete with each other. We are at our best when we share. That's why I love acting. You share with the audience what it is to be human.

....

Kate

I was born in 1949 and grew up as an only child in very working class Manchester. Initially in a two up two down, outside toilet, all of that. We moved to a semi-detached house when I was seven. I passed the 11 plus, one of only four from primary school who went to grammar school. That was the thing that really changed my life, going to grammar school, being in the sixth form and eventually going to university.

Why I was drawn to Kate

Kate is very business-like and comes across as clear, structured and very steady. She has had a wide-ranging working life in a variety of social work and management roles including running a care home business with her husband. She is the mother of two boys who are now grown up.

I warmed to the way she has rigorously identified the principles she holds and her determination to apply them. This came across in both her professional and personal life and decisions. Her early work experience exposed her to seriously troubled children, and she took a high level of responsibility at a young age in this field. In later years she has had the experience of caring for the elderly both via her business but also being very hands-on with her own mother's care right up until her death. She has been very clear about how to maintain boundaries for herself, as a mother, a daughter and a professional. This is highly relevant to my own life, and I'm sure to many women's lives too.

At the time of our conversation, she was enjoying a more relaxed sense of her time being more her own than it has been up till now. There was something very liberating about it – a real opportunity opening up to explore old and new interests. I will watch this space with interest!

Her advice to younger women?

Enjoy the moment, grab the opportunities when they are there, don't end up wondering 'what if?'

....

Kitty

*I was born in Derbyshire in 1930. We were quite a close family.
My grandfather was a very Edwardian, Victorian chappie – he
ruled the family. My husband and I knew each other when
we were teenagers. Being local, our families all knew each
other. We were at school together, the grammar school, and
our families were at church together. It was very much a local
community. So I've lived in this area all the time.*

Why I was drawn to Kitty

Kitty is a keen and accomplished gardener and I first met
her when her garden was open to the public. It is a beautiful,
traditional, very English garden.

She reflects the essence of Englishness herself too. Elegant,
gentle, modest and kind, she exudes a calm discipline. In
conversation, I realised that there was, as I had half expected,
a determined strength, belied by her quietly self-effacing
demeanour. Mother to six children, five of whom survived
to adulthood, she supported her husband's political and
business career and has been (and still is) tirelessly involved in
community and voluntary work.

After school, she studied domestic science in Sheffield which
led to a brief but delightful sounding career as a cookery advisor
with Cadburys, travelling all over the UK (with chocolate).
She shows no bitterness but I couldn't help wondering what
the path not taken might have been like had she been allowed
by her grandfather to take up her desired place to study in
Edinburgh instead.

Contracting oesophageal cancer fourteen years ago, she
recovered and went on to climb Mont Blanc at the age of sixty

nine, raising money for the oesophageal cancer charity in the process.

I came away realising that the strength that some women have is sometimes far from obvious. Kitty's toughness is wrapped in such a classic and feminine exterior that it would be easy to overlook. It was very appealing and seemed to suggest, gently but firmly, that we really should attempt to 'keep calm and carry on'. I find that to be a useful message at times.

Her advice to younger women?

Try to be optimistic. Try to see the good in everything. Look after your health and your appearance as far as possible. I personally find that a strong faith is very helpful in overcoming difficulties – it helped me to recover after cancer. So if you're lucky enough to have found a faith – nurture it!

....

Lesley

I was born in Lancashire (now Merseyside) in 1950. Just after the war. When I was little I used to think the war was a long time ago but it wasn't. As a child, it was my parents' business. It's only quite recently that I've begun to think that it did shape me in all sorts of ways. It shaped the physical conditions that I saw around me, why the town I grew up in was so run down, with derelict bits of land everywhere, my parents' attitudes ... for my parents, actually, it was their golden era.

Why I was drawn to Lesley

I have known Lesley and done some work with her over many years. This conversation was different to those we had previously had though. Once again, it showed that we very rarely ask the people we know what matters and what doesn't.

One of four sisters, one of whom died as a young woman, she was raised in a community that had its roots in the area for generations. She left home to go to university and settled in Nottingham with her partner and son. She has always juggled work in what would now perhaps be called a portfolio career, combining roles in different Higher Educational settings.

Lesley is intelligent, self-deprecating and has no time for pretention. She will always challenge stereotypes and I came away from our conversation with a really interesting insight into the mixed feelings that being part of a 'transition generation' can bring. She sensed her mother's frustrations and had the opportunity to live a very different kind of life for herself but this adjustment hasn't always been easy. I found it reassuring to listen to.

My background is half a generation different, and placed in a different part of the country – but I recognised the long term nature of the changes that many women are living through. What it means to be educated, to move away from your birth family, to have different expectations but the same roots as your family – these are all things that are familiar to me and many of my friends. The conversation was a fascinating exploration of these themes.

Her advice to younger women?

My ten year rule – keep that 'horrible' photo because when you look back at it in ten years' time it will look much better!

More seriously, never think you've left something too late, that the chance has passed you by. You can do it but allow yourself space to learn and to make mistakes.

....

Liberty

I'm so much the result of both my parents. My mother came from the slums in Derby, left home at 14, went into service, ended up in Rochdale as a bar maid. Her family was plagued by the most terrible mental health - lifetimes in institutions, suicides. Shocking, terrible. My father couldn't be more different. He came from a German, Jewish, engineering family, tremendously distinguished. They formed their own business in Manchester, it was immensely successful, but he had made a bad marriage and was very unhappy. He was drinking in this bar where my mother worked. And so these two backgrounds got together. I was born in Stockport in 1946.

Why I was drawn to Liberty
I met Liberty at a New Year workshop designed to help us reflect on the past year and set aspirations for the coming year. Feisty, creative and outspoken, I knew immediately that I wanted her to be part of this project. Awarded a Royal Academy art award in 2011, she works as an artist as well as putting in hours of voluntary work to her local community in Nottingham.

Her unconventional, serious and spirited approach to her work and life came through loud and clear in our conversation, which took place in her kitchen and allowed me to see her work when we took a tour of her studio. Her earlier life involved working as an actor for many years whilst bringing up her son on her own. Re-located, re-married and with a new career direction, she clearly has no time to waste. She has a keen eye for injustice and a huge energy for addressing it. At the same time as this, I sensed an invigorating and playful mischievousness which makes me smile.

Much of our conversation set my creative impulses stirring. Whilst our fields are very different, some of the themes behind her work and this book overlap. I felt emboldened by our conversation, keen to get home and start writing. No time to waste.

Her advice to younger women?

Follow your heart. It will bring adversity, pain, grief and great joy. For self-knowledge and the ways of the world there is nothing to beat it.

....

Linda

I was born in Nottingham in 1945, the eldest of five. Dad worked at the Raleigh bicycle factory, later on he was a foreman in the paint shop. My mum always did a part time job. She worked in Wallis, C&A, a café. I came from a working class home, nobody owned their own house. We lived in a council house which was brand new when we went in it. I left school at fifteen and went to work in a lingerie factory.

Why I was drawn to Linda

Linda is in some ways a larger than life character – an entertaining speaker, a forceful advocate for women, and an energetic organiser. She has raised over £500,000 for charity over the years, and held a variety of influential jobs, with her eventual education in sociology and education. But when I listened to her, I saw a much more vulnerable side – a troubled history of relationships, some real tragedies amongst her friends and family, and a long term sense of trying to live up to her beloved father's ambitions for her (which, as ambitions often are, were born of his own experience. His education was limited by *his* parents who turned down a scholarship he'd won as a teenager, insisting he went to work like his brothers had).

I had met her once or twice at local business events, but didn't know her well. I was particularly impressed with how she had engaged in education later on, when the odds were stacked against her as mother of two small girls and no support from her husband at the time. She has taken jobs and opportunities that she freely admitted she felt terrified about. She is a striking example of someone who hasn't let fear hold her back, and has truly gone the extra mile in encouraging other women to do the same.

Her advice for younger women?

Be kind to yourself, forgive yourself for not being perfect (nobody is – and those who think they are, are boring people). Enjoy being young and don't be too concerned with how you look because you will look back and realise you were lovely and fresh. Take time to care for others less fortunate than yourself.

Madeline

I was born in 1949 in New Zealand. I was born into a – well, New Zealand doesn't have a class system – but I was born into a working family. Both my parents worked, my father was a labourer and so was my mother. I was the youngest child. My eldest sister was 17 years older than me. I was a surprise!

Why I was drawn to Madeline

I hadn't met Madeline before. I knew she and her husband had worked as missionaries and, never having met anyone with that title before, I was fascinated to find out what her take on ageing was going to be. I wasn't disappointed. Her feisty, intellectual independence came across immediately and as the conversation went on, I discovered an impish sense of humour too.

Her work had often centred in countries torn by conflict and the courage she had demonstrated in some hair-raising situations – including teaching boy soldiers and narrowly surviving a plane crash – was way beyond my experience. These experiences, amongst others including bringing up two daughters in the red light district of Amsterdam, led to a determined curiosity to understand what she had witnessed especially in relation to children, power and communication. She is currently pursuing her interests in how we listen to children through a PhD, as well as on a very immediate level by enjoying her role as a grandmother.

The conversation left me feeling inspired about how she has managed to be on a mission (literally in her case) as well as combine a very committed family life and lifelong study. The energy and direction that having a clear purpose seems to bring was very evident.

Her advice to younger women?
I think that we can all learn from each other. I think that it is in intergenerational interactions where there is respect for the experiences of both the younger and older that advice emerges, and is constructed.

....

Margaret

I was born in Wormley in Hertfordshire in 1939. I was wanted and loved, not rich by any means but we weren't desperately poor, and into a rural environment. My Dad had a butcher's shop. Mum had some education in that she had secretarial/ book-keeping training, but never really used it because after her mother died, she was looking after her father and her deaf brother. So neither of my parents really got to where they could or should have done.

Why I was drawn to Margaret
She's my mum!

Possibly enough said, but the reason I wanted to include her was that it can be difficult to see our mothers as anything other than our mothers. There's no getting away from that in the end – the relationship is just as important as the individual identities – but it has been interesting I think from both our perspectives to be doing this project.

Margaret didn't work outside the home when my younger brother and I were young but was soon supporting my newly self-employed father and did so all along, as book-keeper and essential organiser of his more creative impulses. They have very complementary business skills.

When she was about to turn fifty she said to me at New Year that she was about to 'break out' – and allegedly I said, 'Oh, I've heard that before'. My shamefully underwhelming support was apparently the spur to sign up for a full time degree programme in Public Policy and Public Management. If the intention was to 'show me', it worked.

I was, and still am, impressed. She'd left school at sixteen and had little support or opportunity to get a career off the ground. I know she would have made a much better accountant than I was. She used those skills to good effect in years of voluntary work with the United Reformed Church, only very recently having retired from her financial role there.

Her advice for younger women?
Be your own person, try to fulfil your own potential but do not become so single-minded that you ignore or forget those around you. Have some sense of duty and responsibility but do not become weighed down with trying to be all things to all people.

....

Marie

I was born in 1949 and grew up in Essex. I'm the youngest of five. My father was a solicitor. He was the first of his family to go into the professions. He made a big step up by marrying the boss's daughter - one way to do it! He had his own practice. My mother was quite an exceptional woman for her time. She was highly intellectual, on the fringes of the Bloomsbury set. The two big passions for her were education and women.

Why I was drawn to Marie

I didn't know Marie before we met. We share some career history as we both worked for the same 'Big Four' firm of accountants although our paths didn't cross. Marie was a partner, I was much more junior, and we were in different offices. She left the firm in 2002 and now supports, trains and champions women through her consultancy practice.

I was keen to meet her as there aren't many women who have had the career success that she has had and, having some familiarity with the organisation that she worked for, I was curious about what it was really like. When we met, I was immediately drawn to her rebellious spirit and her very reflective and thoughtful style.

She rejected formal education early on and was fiercely independent. She headed to London to make her own way in the world at the age of eighteen, with a job as a council rent collector in Paddington, and was married to her first husband by twenty. She describes him as very working class and very bright. They decided together to go back into formal education in their twenties. Discovering a facility with numbers, she joined her brother-in-law's small regional accountancy practice, which was eventually absorbed into a much bigger firm. Her career ladder was unplanned.

Her intelligence, determination and humour are striking. I came away feeling that I wanted to be more rebellious myself, shake things up a little. I knew that I would have been completely intimidated by her had I met her when I was younger. But now? Not intimidated but inspired. The conversation made me realise how far I have come in those years too.

Her advice for younger women?

*Find whatever process that will help you on the journey to
knowing yourself and recognising what it is in you that inhibits
you from being who you truly can be.*

....

Nicole

*I was born in 1947. My parents were academics and I lived all
over the place, including Canada. I spent my first six years here
in Cambridge, Massachusetts.*

Why I was drawn to Nicole

Nicole and I haven't actually met but it is testament to the
power of the internet that we have connected through our
writing and work. She is a consultant psychiatrist and author in
the United States. We carried out our conversation via Skype.
Personally, whilst I sometimes feel slightly besieged by the
overwhelming nature of the global social network, I find this
kind of connection really exciting. It is truly amazing what we
can use it to achieve.

Nicole's informed and grounded approach to her practice as
a psychiatrist has impressed me. When it came to this project, I
was keen to include her. I felt sure she would have some sound
advice and reflection. I was right.

As a working mother, she has combined similar work to
mine with a similar home set up. Her two children are older
than mine – she has been there and done that with a job that
involves a lot of listening to people and she writes as well. I
came away from our conversation feeling reassured that I am

doing all right. It's a message we all need to hear from time to time I think. It was very calming.

Her advice to younger women?
Don't waste time trying to be too perfectionist about small stuff. Don't think that people really care whether things like dinner parties were perfect. Try not to torture the people you love.

....

Pat

I was born in 1940 in Colchester. My grandparents had a shop, a little general store. There were two or three houses near it, my parents lived in one, my aunt and uncle in another and my grandparents lived above the shop.

Why I was drawn to Pat
I know of Pat through her writing, having heard her read some of her work. Her wry look at life belies her quietly spoken, reserved demeanour. Happily married from a young age – she married at eighteen – she and her husband have three children and six grandchildren. Living in Colchester all her life, she started work at a local calendar factory and worked in a school canteen and as a home help whilst her children were young.

Adult education classes led to a philosophy degree in her forties. Always interested in creative writing (and with a real talent for it from what I can tell), she tells me she has a novel in the drawer. I hope one day it emerges into the bookshops.

My conversation with her left me filled with the sense of contentment that Pat projects. Happy with her own company, and good friends with her husband over such a long marriage, she speaks and writes lovingly of her family. She doesn't appear to be striving to be, or to have, something else in the way that so many people seem to.

This conversation was a real reminder that often what we need is right here with us all along.

Her advice to younger women?

Don't drag your feet if there is something you really want to do and, if you have children, always try to answer their questions honestly as and when they ask them. Don't fob them off.

....

Rose

I was born in 1927 in Durban, South Africa. I was an only child. The school they sent me to was 300 miles away. It took two days to get there. During the war nobody had much petrol so I used to go on a bus for a day and change on to a train and eventually get there. I was 13. It was a state school, so it wasn't posh, they had to have state boarding schools [in South Africa] because farmer's children lived thirty miles or more away.

Why I was drawn to Rose

I know of Rose as a writer and have seen her perform with her writing group. She is adventurous, impatient and energetic. Her writing is filled with dry humour and wicked observation. I would describe her as something of a tonic.

She married an English doctor after attending Natal University College, and they went on to have four children before moving to the UK because of his work. She didn't work a great deal whilst the children were young but then taught part time at the local college. She describes herself as not being terribly ambitious. Widowed at 59, and sadly losing one of her children as a young adult too, she has gone on to live a very independent life, travelling extensively, playing tennis and enjoying a wide range of cultural activities.

I believe that any woman would be impressed by Rose. More active than many women decades younger than herself, she is a real inspiration in terms of showing the value of staying fit and interested in many things. I came away from our conversation feeling a real sense of possibility – perhaps not that *anything* is possible but certainly it's worth having a go. Age and difficult life events aren't barriers for her, and I suspect this mind-set is as important as good genes or physical fitness. It's very encouraging to witness.

Her advice for younger women?
Keep running around and don't give up anything until you have to.

....

Simran

I was born in India, in the Punjab, in 1954. I came to England by ship with my parents and older brother. My parents have often talked fondly of that journey as an experience never to be forgotten. It took about two months. My father owned a clothes and cosmetics store in Patiala; it was the first shop in the area to have glass fronted windows. He had

travelled to England in 1950 to export cosmetics; it was
during this visit that he decided he wanted to make a life
here. He studied at Aston University and obtained a degree in
mechanical engineering having left India as a pilot. He is a real
entrepreneur having owned businesses from petrol stations
to dry cleaning. He instilled his forward thinking values in his
seven children.

Why I was drawn to Simran

Simran was introduced to me by one of my other interviewees.
She is the youngest of the twenty women, at the time of the
conversation falling just under my lower age limit of sixty, but
was suggested as someone with 'an old soul'. I was intrigued.

Her adult life has been dominated by caring responsibilities.
Hers was an arranged marriage. Her family was unaware
that Huntingdon's disease ran in her husband's family. Now
widowed after many years of caring for him, she cares for her
daughter who has juvenile Huntingdon's disease.

Throwing herself into work as a business woman, managing
teams of community development workers and later as a
lecturer and life coach, she achieved a variety of senior roles, as
well as raising three children. She used her experience as a carer
to be a non-executive director on the Primary Care Trust for
many years. She now spends as much time writing as she can.

Listening to her, I was forcibly struck by what a tough hand
she had been dealt. But it also made me reflect on the research[1]
which points out that our circumstances are not everything
when it comes to happiness. Our mindset and attitudes play
a bigger role than most of us realise in how content we feel.
Simran, not in great health herself, is a living example of this. It
was a humbling reminder to me.

Her advice to younger women?

Look after your health. It is your number one asset which we tend to take for granted. Listen to and follow your intuition. Enjoy living in the moment. The past is a cancelled cheque, tomorrow is a promissory note, today is ready cash. Use it.

....

Tanje

I was born in 1944. I was very premature, worryingly so. My mother was exceedingly ill. I think it was very touch and go. I think that coloured the fact that they didn't have any more children. My father loved children, he never really grew up. Huge sense of fun. I had an incredibly strict mum and also a career mum – she was extremely focused on her career which was very unusual for her time. She passed the eleven plus for the grammar school but wasn't allowed to go because they couldn't afford the uniform. It never left her so she was determined to get on and do something. She went to evening classes and then went into the Civil Service and did all the exams, all the levels, against all odds. We shared a home with my grandparents in London.

Why I was drawn to Tanje

Tanje is sociable and gregarious. I had met her once or twice socially. Hugely energetic and a great organiser, she comes across as the life and soul of the party. Our conversation revealed an interesting life: trained as a teacher, she then taught expatriates' children in an oil company in Iran where she met her husband and then travelled around Europe with his job. Two children later, they settled in the Netherlands where she worked for the British Embassy. They have now retired back to the UK where they are busier than ever with community roles and projects.

Our conversation had me laughing a lot of the time. Tanje has many entertaining stories from the places she has lived in and the wide variety of people she has met. She spoke very honestly and positively about the value of allowing each other to be yourselves within long term relationships and marriage. It has clearly worked well in her case and I received the impression that this didn't happen by accident, but was something she and her husband had negotiated and worked at over the years. Her strong principles about how she believes people should be treated also came across, with examples of how she has challenged authority on occasions. A woman with many friends, she is a good illustration of the value of a strong network, and the effort needed to maintain it.

I came away with a spring in my step from our conversation. There is much to laugh at and much to enjoy. Long may it last.

Her advice to younger women?
Give and take but remain true to yourself especially in relationships. Always stand up for injustice however unpopular it may prove to be.

....

Val

I was born in 1950 in Birmingham, the only child to elderly parents. My dad was ten years older than my mother and my mother didn't have me till she was 39. Very happy background, very supportive parents. You never know as an only child if you're spoilt, but I think I'm spoilt in love and support and encouragement. Traditional background, he came home from work, meal on the table, mother never worked.

Why I was drawn to Val

I didn't know Val before we met. She and her husband have had long and successful careers as secondary school teachers (her in art, him in history), as well as bringing up two sons. She is now devoting herself to her work as a textile artist.

She was very easy to chat to. Cheerful and practical, she left me with a real sense of possibility about nurturing creativity. Her example has shown that it's achievable throughout (and sometimes because of) all the other things that may come our way including jobs, child-care and caring for elderly parents. Val understood well the frustrations of just getting started on things when you get called away to do something else (the experience of so many women) but also is a living demonstration of what can happen when you never give up trying. She is now beginning to make a real impact as an artist with exhibitions and invitations to show her work.

I found her 'can do' spirit to be highly infectious.

Her advice to younger women?

Go for it! Have the confidence not to waste a minute and have the confidence in yourself to achieve anything you want to.

CHAPTER 1

AN INCREASING SENSE OF URGENCY

No time to waste – deferred gratification – being a good old person – retirement – invisible? – what matters – what doesn't

....

My children are away this week. One is working as a lifeguard at a festival. The other is on a school residential trip. At the time of writing, they are sixteen and fourteen years old.

I have no worries about them. As far as I know, they are safe and happy. Emergency contact details have been dispensed. The universe is in order as they begin the long process of fleeing the nest. And I have been looking forward to a few days of uninterrupted time to myself.

The urgency is flashing like a red hot beacon. Make the most of it. No time like the present. Do all those things you normally don't have time for.

I stare back at the urgency as if it is a forbidden vice, suddenly revealed. It's like being left in a bank vault and being told you can help yourself. I am paralysed and restless. I'm not sure what the rules are, or whether there are any. What should I expect from myself? I have a dread of wasting the opportunity, of wasting time.

At the same time I discover I am tired. Exhausted. I crave a holiday, sunshine, a retreat. Maybe a cake, or a drink.

I'm also bored. *But I'm never bored*, I say to myself. I usually have boundless enthusiasm for a whole host of things. Suddenly unrestricted, it seems to have evaporated. I feel as if I have fallen through the back of the wardrobe. This is a taste of an unknown country.

I want to explore. I feel an unreliable energy fizzing and popping whilst an underlying inertia rolls in nauseous waves. Perhaps I want to go to bed. *In the daytime??*

Is it hormones? Being the menopausal mother of adolescent girls, we live in the House of Hormones. Usefully at times, there are few things that can't be blamed on these mysterious substances. Perhaps I am experiencing a hormonal surge that accompanies my children venturing out into the world. Something like ripping a plaster off. The flood of pain is followed by a rush of calming chemicals that inform me this is really *all right*.

Or is it a foretaste of the so-called Empty Nest Syndrome? Well, perhaps, though that is a little melodramatic as they are coming back on Thursday. The first question will be *what's for tea?* I love being a mother but the housekeeper aspects can be trying. I know I can be irritable with catering, washing, lifts and nagging, mostly all at speed and in volume.

And then the question looms at me. *Is this impatient inactivity a sign of ageing?*

Perhaps it has little to do with my children. Perhaps it is compounded by biological upheaval, which affects all women, mothers or not. Perhaps it has to do with realising I am almost certainly *more than half way* through my life. Perhaps this is just how it is.

No time to waste

I was about 49 or 50 and I was waiting to speak in a meeting. I suddenly thought, actually I know what I'm talking about. Why am I expecting other people to be more knowledgeable? I realised, I'm at the age now when they should be thinking that about me. I thought, I've wasted a bit of time here.
—Jeannie

I've seen so many things, like my friend dying of cancer, that make me realise you have to live for the day. I have an urgency. I don't have time to worry about things that might never happen.
—Val

At 63 you can almost start again. So there's another whole big question for me – start again at what? Do I want to? And I don't mean this morbidly at all, but have I done enough?
—Marie

It's a truism but as my forties progress, I am increasingly conscious that there is not as much time left as there was. I know people my age who are contemplating (or starting to long for) retirement. I also know of sad instances of premature illness and death amongst my contemporaries.

I can clearly remember things that happened forty years ago. I'll be lucky to have another healthy and active forty years. *I'd better get started then.*

This provokes a deluge of emotions: panic, excitement and ennui. The quiet rebel in me stirs at the thought of doing something unexpected and adventurous. The calmer inner self observes the turmoil. The mother in me wonders how realistic it is to expect to get started, and the daughter in me wonders if childcare will be instantly replaced with elder care. And the wave of ennui comes as I ask, get on with *WHAT?*

At this age it is clearly too late for some things. When I was a teenager, despite sometimes overwhelming angst, I had a sense of the world being my oyster. It felt as if I could potentially do anything, live anywhere, be whatever I liked.

Now, however, my perception has changed. Whilst I still believe there is a great deal of potential, I understand better now that life is a series of decisions. We have to choose one course of action over another, even if that choice is inaction. This was true as a teenager but it didn't feel like that. I also know that my energy is not an infinite resource any more than my time is – again, not that it ever was in reality.

At this mid-life moment, I am feeling rather like a school-leaver. I could do anything. Or nothing. It alarms me that by choosing one path you eliminate others. It is easy to put it all off by dithering around doing things that don't matter much at all. There's never any shortage of *stuff* to fill time.

In the space of a few days, I don't resolve this confusion of drives and emotions. I spend the time doing a few chores *(bored)*; some interviews for this book *(excited)*; some nurturing time *(phew)* and quite a lot of wondering what's going on *(curious)*. It is, as expected, drawn to a close by *what's for tea?* There's some relief in knowing the answer. Macaroni cheese.

The conversations show me that this mixed sense of urgency is not my unique experience. On the plus side, it definitely does help to galvanise me into action. As my teenagers might say, 'YOLO' – You Only Live Once being the justification for doing whatever you feel like, it seems to me. It can be convenient and liberating.

But on the downside, this urgency can lead to a darker place. An anxious driven state, where it is possible to run yourself ragged trying to fit a massive range of activities into overstuffed diaries. I know that our life can definitely feel like that on occasions and I am wary of overcommitting as a result. Even when these are enjoyable, interesting, fun activities, it can feel a little like eating too many sweets. The net result for me is that I can't remember or savour anything much that is going on.

This less helpful side of the urgency equation is influencing all age groups I suspect. As the anti-ageing message is increasingly targeted at those barely out of their childhood, there is a danger that this perceived pressure to live life to the full *at all times* can lead to flipping between frantic activity and paralysing inertia.

Deferred gratification

I've spent a great deal of my life saying, 'When I get to be..., when I am..., when this or that happens...' And this is it. This is the life. It could have been at 30, 40, 50, 20 – some people grasp it a lot earlier than I did. This is the time when I don't say, oh, I'll do that later. I'll do it now.
—Helen

I hate the concept of the 'bucket list' – a list of places to visit or things to do before you die – as it seems to encompass everything that is driven and anxious about urgency. Some of the very best things in life happen when you stumble upon them unexpectedly.

It is not possible to do everything, and it is not possible to do everything *right now*. I have reconciled myself to the fact that there are more good books than I will ever have time to read, more interesting places than I will ever visit, more interesting people than I will ever meet. I have always had more ideas than time. At least this means there's little danger of running out.

However, I do think it is important to recognise what I might be saving for some imaginary future filled with time and resources. For me, writing used to be in that category. It was something I would do when I had more time. Fortunately, a whole variety of events, including unwelcome ones like a global recession, led me to my notebook.

It is about consciously acknowledging our priorities and acting upon them. If we prioritise our friendships, or exercise, or a hobby, it means putting them into our busy weeks first, before everything else fills the diary. If we *really* want to do something, we can usually find a way of doing it.

Along with many of the women I spoke to, I have been brought up to see the benefits in deferring gratification. The famous Stanford University marshmallow experiment and other follow up studies were the first to illustrate this[2]. Children who can be left alone in a room with a sweet or other treat on the promise that if they don't eat it the researcher will return with two, tend to do better in later years at school and work.

I suspect I would have been good at that exercise as a young child. I was always good at making things last, and saving the best till last. My mother could have taken this to international competition levels. For her, rationing during and after the Second World War has been a very real influence in teaching her to wait – for a long time – for good things. It could be argued that there has been a swing too far back the other way for later generations.

My life has been about deferred gratification in some significant ways – education (putting in years of slog at times for later results and opportunities) and money (being urged to save for pensions and rainy days) being the key ones. There is a lot of sense and value in this (well, not sure about the pension minefield).

But it can spill over into other areas which are less logical. We may not wear the clothes we like the most because we save them for best. We may not use indulgent gifts we are given because we save them for special occasions. We may not even eat some particularly good ingredients because we save them until they go off. I've done all of those things.

I am reminded of a friend who sadly told me about finding unopened luxury bath products in her mother's bathroom cabinet after she died. We probably all know of people who waited for retirement to fulfil long held ambitions and then became ill or died before they got the chance. There is a uniquely individual balance to be struck. We all have to find the right balance for ourselves.

But I wonder whether mid-life might be the point at which this deferred gratification balance tips in favour of eating your sweets now rather than waiting to see if someone brings you another one. Figuratively of course.

Being a good old person

I think there are things about being an older person that can be a pressure. There is this pressure to be doing something. I don't know what, but you won't be sitting around doing nothing. You'll be travelling, you'll be doing something important, using the benefits of your accumulated wisdom, whatever it is, for the good of the world. There is a pressure – to be a good old person.
—Lesley

Nothing angers me more, it makes me grit my teeth,
this assumption that you're over sixty so you are in this
homogeneous group, all pensioners.
—Kate

What does older age look like for women from this generation onwards? Quite simply, I don't think we know. The generation of women I have spoken to are in the first significant wave of women, freed from the constraints of large families and a wholly patriarchal culture, to be shaping it. And it won't be the same for all of them – why on earth would we expect that it would be?

Some will want to do 'good works', some will want to be hell-raisers, some will want to watch daytime television, some will want to earn and some will want to devote themselves to their grandchildren. And everything you can think of besides. In short, they won't stop being people. There are increasing numbers of women who are in the public eye who are now reaching their fifties, sixties and beyond. It seems wrong to me that many of them are now in the spotlight by virtue of their age rather than their profession or expertise.

Meanwhile, older men in the public eye seem simply to carry on doing whatever they are skilled at and interested in, and we all carry on paying attention whilst we still respect and value what they are doing. Many of them are undeniably well worth paying attention to. But the contribution of older women is so often obscured by discussion of their appearance or by judgements about whether they are 'good for their age'. Women as often as men seem to be leading these discussions and judgements too, I might add. We can be our own worst enemy.

I am unaware that, beyond the law, there are any rules about how we should be at a certain age (men or women, but women may be only just realising this). It can make life tricky in terms of not having strict conventions to follow, and does require us to think harder than we might have done in past centuries. But how immensely liberating.

Retirement

I heard myself say to someone, oh, I've retired. And I Hate. That. Word. It sounds as if your life is shutting down.
—Val

It isn't about retirement, for me, it's about changing my working life pattern. Now, more than half of what I do, I do for nothing. The whole idea was that this is the time when you give something back to society and I'm quite happy to do that.
—Jane

I used to say I was retired and people would ask me what I meant. I started saying, well, actually, I'm running an assisted living facility – I'd got my elderly mother, a dog that was going blind, my youngest son and his girlfriend had just moved back in with us, my husband was working very long hours and my elderly mother-in-law lives in the next road...
—Kate

The conversations highlighted just how artificial the notion of retirement can be, especially for women. It's a cliff edge that accompanies the ending of useful contribution in terms of the Western capitalist model. By and large, it seems to be a construct of the Industrial Revolution, where people are literally used up by decades of hard graft keeping meals on the table. For anyone who has been working in that way (and millions of people still do), I suspect the notion of just stopping – retiring – has a genuine appeal.

But for most of the women I spoke to, life was much more complex than this. Paid work was one thread but bringing up families, caring, voluntary work, creative work, housework and learning were all equally part of the picture. Some aspects took centre stage at some stages of life, others at other times. There was a sense of ebb and flow about this – which I can entirely relate to.

Even the women who had worked full time in demanding careers over many years didn't show much sign of wanting or needing to retire in an exhausted heap, fit for little more than tending to the wounds inflicted during that time.

These women (and I) are lucky to have been born in times and circumstances where we haven't been forced to work in fields or sweatshops simply to survive. Many people have little choice about this. But along with our fortunate life expectancy and education come choices. We are blessed to have those choices but it doesn't necessarily mean they are easy to make.

The traditional model of retirement doesn't seem to suit women well. Many women continue doing the domestic, caring and support roles that they have always done until the day they physically cannot do them anymore. They may do this willingly, resentfully or unquestioningly (or a bit of all three).

In addition, many of the women I listened to feel that they are just coming into their own as they approach traditional retirement age. The accumulated experience both in and outside of the workplace can result in an energetic enthusiasm to get stuck in to new projects. It can be a like a blast of fresh air.

Women's biology may also be a factor. Given the significant transitions that women experience through puberty, childbirth and the menopause, it would be something of a surprise if the majority of women followed a straight line experience of school, work and retirement. And of course, not all women want or are able to work full time in demanding jobs that they may no longer enjoy into their sixties, seventies and beyond (the same applies to men). As several of the women discussed, it is about being able to adjust the pattern of their working lives as a new phase arrives.

Many women are already skilled at this kind of adjustment. They have often transformed their working patterns, sometimes several times, to fit around other commitments and their understanding of where their skills are best used. Through long experience, older women often have a clear and energetic sense of what issues need to be addressed, and possess a keen desire to address them. They frequently find ways to express their own perhaps long frustrated creativity, regardless of their age.

It doesn't sound like shutting down to me.

Invisible?

What do people mean about older women being invisible? I don't understand that at all. Not mattering any more is about not being visible to yourself *isn't it?*
—Anne

I remember learning to ski. The guys were bombing around and an older woman I'd made friends with looked at me and said, follow me, we don't need to do it their way. And I thought, yay.... We're still going to do it but we're not going to do it their way. It was such a wonderful piece of wisdom.
—Marie

I think to some extent, my dad overshadowed my mum. I saw she was far more knowledgeable and intelligent than I'd realised – not that I ever thought she wasn't, she was certainly on the ball. But there were things she came out with, politically and in other ways, after he died, that I'd never heard before.
—Linda

For centuries, many women have been seen and not heard, in the home and in public life. Stepping outside of the home, many have made valiant and often very successful attempts to compete on men's terms, which have sometimes come at a great cost. Others have denied or subsumed their own interests, or simply never had a chance to find out what their own interests really are.

As they get older, sadly many women are overlooked. This happens in the media but also in other more mundane interactions such as getting served in shops and cafes. My 'bar presence', never great, is already diminishing as the years pass. I'm going to have to come up with some dramatic strategies at this rate to get a drink when I'm seventy.

In my experience, my friends and I do not seem to have relationships with partners or husbands that mean we are put down or our opinions are dismissed at home, but in public and work settings we are not yet old enough to know whether or how this will affect us. Has there been a cultural shift for all women, in all arenas? I think it would be dangerous to assume so.

Education helps. And over time, my hope is that men *and* women are growing in confidence both to do things in their own way and, importantly, to accept other approaches. It takes confidence to do that too, instead of mocking, ignoring or attacking others' methods if they are different from our own.

Many of the women I spoke to knew of female friends and relatives whose experience was one of being constantly undermined or put down by the men they lived with. Whether it's through custom, expectation, tacit collusion or bullying, one form of older women's invisibility seems to come about as a result of their relationships with the men in their lives. In the end it can mean that the women themselves join in, putting themselves down and believing they no longer matter. Not surprisingly, such patterns can be associated with depression. I wonder how much it diminishes the men too.

Perhaps it happens gradually. Maybe the man automatically drives when a couple gets into the car. Perhaps the man controls the bank account, or has the last say on financial decisions. Maybe when one half of a couple is used to being the boss at work, this carries over into home relationships and dynamics – and statistically this is more likely to be the man. Perhaps the woman has had time out of the workplace and has lost confidence in that sphere for a while, and that has not been addressed in the relationship. Maybe it's just the result of different personalities, or historical roles that were adopted early on in the relationship and have never been questioned.

People disagree over whether they think that invisibility is an issue for older women or not. I've had some interesting conversations about this outside of those I've carried out for this book. It seems to boil down to individual women's experience and I think it's very encouraging that I have met plenty of women who feel as visible as the men they live and work with.

My reflection is that invisibility is partly to do with other people's attitudes and partly to do with how we, as older women, collude with that. I think there are particular issues for women in the public eye which probably require collective challenge. Finding the strength and energy to resist the bias that we may encounter isn't always easy.

It may be a trivial thing, but I've been tempted to give up at some bars or ask someone younger or – well – more *male* to buy drinks with my money on my behalf. I sometimes fear this might be just the beginning. We need to watch out for each other.

....

WHAT MATTERS

- Identifying priorities
- Acting on priorities
- Supporting each other
- Being adaptable

WHAT DOESN'T

- Bucket lists
- Saving the best till last
- Assuming there is a right way to be an older woman
- Fixed concepts of retirement

CHAPTER 2
PATINA

Shape-shifting – maintenance – hair – clothes – extreme measures – perspective and dining tables – what matters – what doesn't

....

The mail arrived whilst I was out. I picked it up as I was turning off the house alarm, hanging up my coat, and thinking about the perennial question of what's for tea.

Ta Dah! The leaflet fell out of the envelope, with loyalty point vouchers for a range of moisturisers I often use. As I reached for my purse, absently wondering where to put them so that I would remember to use them, I took a second look.

Clinically proven anti-ageing technology, tailored for 45-60 year old skin.

I know what the point of this loyalty scheme is. In a way I am quite pleased about specific marketing based on what they know about me. It cuts down the choice when faced with a baffling shelf full of alternatives. And – don't get me wrong – I like decent skin care products.

But the phrase 'anti-ageing' niggles. I look closer. The range suggested for my age group is highlighted. It tells me I will see younger skin in a few weeks with regular use. I look at the descriptions for other age ranges. It promises to delay the first fine lines for women aged 25 to 35. For women of 60+, the promise is for skin that looks and feels younger.

In some ways I have no problem with any of this. The claims are very carefully worded and don't seem particularly outrageous. Most of us want our skin to be in good condition. Young skin is lovely. I am sure I'm not the only woman to have gazed wistfully at my children's skin from time to time. I will probably buy the suggested products.

My discomfort arises from the assumptions inherent in the marketing campaign, and many others like it. That *of course* women want to look younger than they really are. And that looking young is the only way to look beautiful.

The implication is that all of us are (or perhaps should be) scared of time passing. This fear is stealthily fostered in many areas of our modern lives. Throughout, the reality ticks away. We might look healthy, stylish, or indeed beautiful, but age only goes in one direction. We all know it.

When did everything start having *anti-ageing* on the label? What comes first – the demand for these products or the supply? Women seem particularly adept at internalising these messages. I know of women who have asked their husbands for electric gadgets and treatments that promise anti-ageing benefits, or even asked for cosmetic surgery as a post-baby or birthday treat. Some of these things are painful, risky and laborious. I can't help wondering how on earth we have come to this. [A note to my husband if he is reading this: don't go there. Thankfully, I can't imagine for one moment that he would consider it.]

Shape-shifting

I warm to the idea that age is just a number, but it's frightening how everything sags, isn't it?
—Jeannie

My body has changed dramatically, partly because of my illness, partly because I've gone through the menopause and partly because it's just what happens. I find the loss of muscle tone is a source of grieving but as a thriver I know that I can get to grips with it.
—Helen

I like myself old. I like my grey hair and my wrinkles. I like my flabby bum and floppy tummy. Floppy tits. I don't quite know why, but I didn't like myself when I was young, pretty, attractive, sexy.
—Liberty

In recent years, my body has reached a new stage which is a challenge to my habitual low maintenance outlook. There has been a shift in the distribution of fat, as well as a distinctly new tone and diminishing elasticity of my skin. Efficient hand driers now hold a horrible fascination as I watch the skin being ruffled up like fabric under the jet of warm air. This doesn't happen to my daughters, and it does happen to my mother (I've done some observations in motorway service stations). We all laugh. Then wordlessly move on to the café.

I have reached the menopause relatively early. I know that this has brought about physical changes which I can't help being startled and sometimes a little distressed about. My life-long dependable shape and weight has become unreliable. It has happened quite quickly. It's something over which I have minimal control. My shape and weight were not things I gave much thought to in my younger years. I was far too busy wishing I was shorter.

Now, knowing that my unsurprisingly tall daughters sometimes have similarly painful struggles with accepting their height, I realise that the *only* option is to focus on ways to come to terms with it. There is no other way if you are not to spend your life miserably longing for something that will never be.

At 5 feet 11 inches, I eventually grasped the fact that it was only awkward for other people when I was awkward about it. If I slouched and hung back waiting for other people to approach me, they usually didn't. Of course, at sixteen, I blamed that entirely on my actual objective height. Tall = no-one wanting to talk to me = no-one likes me (especially boys of course). Therefore, slouch and hang back a bit more. It was a vain attempt to look shorter (it actually makes you look taller), and I'd also shot my confidence to pieces by my assessment of what was going on.

It was such an unhelpful interpretation I want to rush back in time and give myself a big hug and a good talking to. It took me ages to realise that men worth their salt weren't as concerned about it as I was. It also took me ages to realise that if someone comments, it is just that – an observation – not a malicious character assassination.

Recently, I entered a lift with one other woman. She was about eighteen inches shorter than me. The doors shut. We looked at each other. And burst out laughing. No doubt she has experienced as many character-building moments from her end of the scale as I have at this end. It simply is as it is.

I'm doing my best to help my girls arrive at this acceptance in fewer years than the decade or two it took me. I don't know if there are any short (!) cuts. I'm aware that the three of us cannot help but make an entrance when we go into a room together but I'm starting to enjoy that. At last.

I was reminded of all this when I listened to the women. An inevitably ageing appearance requires the same mindset. The choice is whether you pour your energy into wishing your body and face were different, or into coming to terms with them. Neither approach is easy, but it's only the second that will free up your attention to get on with other more interesting things. The irony is that this seems to have the biggest anti-ageing impact of all.

In recent years, my feelings about my changing shape have sometimes led me to lose touch with my underlying belief that the health and functioning of my body is far more important than its appearance. A body and mind that is as healthy, fit and happy as it can be, at any level of age, disability or even illness, has a vitality about it that cannot be bought from the chemist or cosmetic surgeon. The conversations have really helped me to remember that. It takes a bit of getting your head around in our culture. But it can be done.

Maintenance

I think peer pressure is key. The women in my cohort here all have a natural look which is carefully maintained. In order to look that natural you have to have a lot done.
—Nicole

Each time I shed a habit - like dying my hair or using make up – I felt much better. I felt really more centred and happier.
—Liberty

I just don't want to look dowdy. It's not about wanting to look younger.
—Madeline

I've always thought of myself as a low maintenance woman. I don't wear much make-up. I can usually be ready to go out in minutes. I don't often look in mirrors or spend a great deal on beauty treatments. Earlier in my life I might have seen this as a boast, a kind of inverted snobbery.

On closer examination, it is more complex. Yes, I like to think I have other things to do, and also don't want to be thought vain. But I also feel a slightly shameful ignorance. Growing up without sisters, in a household that certainly didn't prioritise appearance (for a mix of reasons including religion, and a lively anti-consumerism message), it felt unseemly to be preoccupied with my appearance.

At the same time, as a teenager, I devoured any top tips shared in *Jackie* magazine, especially those that didn't involve spending money. I've put cucumber on my eyes, lemon on my elbows, tried rinsing my hair in tea and putting oats all over my face. All this furtive activity was shot through with embarrassment that I actually *wanted* to pay attention to my appearance. And if I got past that, the next issue was that I didn't really know how to. I was alternately making it up or trying to ignore it as I went along.

As a result, I don't have much experience of beauty therapists. I have rarely had a facial or manicure. My hairdresser comes to our house, having become a friend over the sixteen years she's been cutting my hair. I'd feel slightly intimidated (and annoyed with myself for that) in a salon. I am found wanting in discussions at make-up counters. I find it uncomfortable to be closely scrutinised and asked, in shocked tones, whether I regularly use eye cream (I have since that particular encounter).

I'm also horrified by the price of good quality make-up and skin care products. It's an effort to appear nonchalant as I hand over my credit card in the way I observe other women doing. *It's because you're worth it* – what??? Really???

But as a result of the conversations, I have a dawning realisation that I am not faced with a stark choice between increasingly expensive and complicated actions or letting myself go. There is some middle ground, rather to my surprise.

The beauty and fashion industry has a way of dishing out rules that I think I respond to more than I'd realised. I've found it useful to have a few rules that very quickly become a touchstone. Examples include: *I must take off all make up before bed*; *I must moisturise my face every day*; *I must use an eye cream.* It goes into the same place in my mind as *I must brush my teeth twice a day.* Clear and simple, these don't require any decisions. Just do it.

As I get older, more and more instructions are being added, gleaned unconsciously from magazines, adverts and overheard conversations. *I must not wear strappy tops at my age*; *I must wear foundation*; *I must use foot and hand cream every day.* Some of these I follow. Some of them I don't – I forget, I can't be bothered, I rebel. They hang around at the back of my mind making me feel guilty, embarrassed and – not worth it.

The conversations have brought this into a conscious place for me, which I am finding very helpful. It turns out that I can choose to wear make-up or not. I can ask about skin care and experiment with what works for me and with what I want (or don't want) to do. I can develop my own style and beauty guidelines (not rules), which will probably change as the years go on.

It's deeply refreshing – and rather calming – not to feel that I am on some unstoppable train, the anti-ageing express. I can get on and off as I choose. Who'd have thought?

Hair

I used to colour my hair when I started to go grey, for years and years. One day we were standing at the counter at the video shop. I looked up at the CCTV screen and saw the back of my head and a silver circle there. And I thought, how sad is that? That was it. Never again. I'd rather 'come out'.
—Liberty

I've left my hair to go grey but then my kids will say 'No mum, please don't.' The pressure comes from them more than from anything else. I'd like to go away for a year so that all of my hair becomes nice and white and then come back when it's done.
—Simran

We went to a concert and I looked across this sea of people and everybody had white hair. No. I can't do it. Some people look fantastic with white hair, don't they? I know I wouldn't. So, it could be this colour until I'm eighty.
—Val

I have been colouring my (brown) hair for a decade or more.
I have tried to keep to my original natural shade as far as
possible, and have always done it myself. I don't enjoy the
process. It's messy, time-consuming, and always induces slight
anxiety that I might suddenly have a violent allergic reaction.
I also vaguely wonder about the impact of washing all those
chemicals down the drain. In addition, during a recent visit to
the optician it was very politely pointed out that the dye was
discolouring the expensive arms of my glasses.

And, no minor point, if I spend an hour a month on average
on buying, thinking about, testing and actually colouring my
hair, over a decade this adds up to 120 hours. *Fifteen* working
days. That's a whole holiday. Fifteen days that my husband,
father and brother have spent resting or working or Doing
Something More Interesting. I hear a penny loudly dropping.
I simply don't want to devote fifteen days in the next decade
to sitting in the bathroom, myopically anxious about the
paintwork, and resentfully pouring chemicals on my head.

However, until very recently, I truly didn't think there
was an alternative. I am not a stupid person. I just assumed
that the received wisdom from friends, the media, fears about
ageing and examples of women around me was somehow
unquestionably right. And therefore I *didn't* really question it.
Going grey is a bad idea *for women* I assumed. It's synonymous
with becoming invisible, past it and letting yourself go. Fade
to grey.

For men, lucky them, it's distinguished. This is, I assumed,
simply the way of the world we live in.

As I write this, I don't know how grey I am. I don't know
whether it is a 'nice' grey or not, which is a common argument.
But how do women know what kind of grey they are? Who

makes these judgements? What exactly is a nice grey, and is it in the eye of the beholder?

Listening to my older women has stripped back these assumptions. It's brought the question of grey into my conscious mind. This means it can be challenged.

It's made me more aware of women I pass in the street or see in cafés and shops. When I see a woman with grey roots to her hair, I see a woman (like me) who feels a pressure to colour her hair but actually is too busy, interesting, poor or pre-occupied to maintain it every day of her life. I don't judge her negatively. In fact it's the very reverse. She probably has better things to do with her time. Hallelujah.

I also see women with pink hair or orange hair or brown, blonde or red hair. Some have grey or white hair that is very short or very long. It can all look fantastic. My hope for any woman is that whatever she chooses, it is a real choice. Let's challenge these sneaky assumptions.

(Post-script: as I go to press, any vestiges of my dyed hair have grown out. I was nervous about telling my hair-dresser what I was doing. She has had me nailed for years as one of her lowest maintenance clients, and I thought she'd see this as evidence of me Going Too Far and try to talk me out of it. I asked her to cut it shorter. She did and I love it. And neither she nor I could believe it but *she didn't notice that it was greyer every time she came*. My unsuspecting husband spilled the beans by wandering past and asking her what she thought of my 'au naturel' colouring. We're now all agreed it's not only fine, but better than it was. And guess what? Lower maintenance than ever. Happy days.)

Clothes

I went out the other night when I thought, I should really wear a classic shirt and trousers. But I thought, sod it. I know I can look grown up but this was a party out on the lawn. So I wore my leggings, a thin tee shirt and a lovely top. People did turn round and look but I don't care. But it is difficult. In two years I'll be seventy, I can't carry on wearing this stuff.
—Cecelia

I would urge every woman to get her colours done. That made a huge difference to me. Lifted my confidence no end. I could wear really beautiful colours and wow, my whole world changed.
—Marie

There is something about older lady dressing that I'm conscious of but I don't know what it is that I shouldn't be dressing in. I look at the ranges in the high street that are aimed at me and I really don't like them. That's what they think I should be wearing.
—Anne

This generation is at the cutting edge, as I've said before. What older women wore in generations past was either dictated by impractical and prescriptive etiquette (for wealthier people – clothes you couldn't walk or sit down in, or needed assistance to put on at all) or all too practical concerns (for the majority of us – homemade clothes that were warm, cheap and would last forever).

These days are past (I think). It can leave older women today all at sea.

Once again, the conversations on this topic were illuminating. There was uncertainty from some of the women, searching around for those elusive but tyrannical rules. This often stemmed from what they thought other people might expect them to wear. Often they knew what they *didn't* want to wear. Quite a few compared themselves (often unfavourably) with other people. And there were some who had reached peace with their own style, whatever that might be.

I've wavered between extremes on this one. It hasn't just been confined to mid-life. I can be in a mindset where I genuinely don't care what I'm wearing as long as I'm warm and comfortable. I also know what it's like to feel suddenly out of place because of my clothes.

One memorable business trip on a distant September day was a particular nadir. Stopped at airport security, my make-up was confiscated, my bag was tipped out for the contents to be scrutinised, and I had to take my shoes off. The queue of regular business commuters behind me was getting impatient. I was getting flustered. Arriving in wet and windy Edinburgh, I realised the summer was over, a detail that had escaped my attention when I got dressed at 4.30am in Nottingham. My bare legs were turning blue. Everyone else had tights and boots on.

Having spent most of the previous few weeks in shorts and tee shirts with the children over the school holidays, I felt sort of unpractised in my work clothes. Buttons kept coming undone. Nothing seemed to sit well. Shoes and clothes were soaking up the rain like blotting paper. Imagine my dismay when I finally got to the meeting to discover everyone else was totally relaxed in jeans and sweatshirts.

Deciding what to wear can feel like walking through a forest in the dark, especially when your body is changing. For women of a certain age of course, this may also mean taking account of the need to be able to strip all unnecessary layers off *as fast as possible* when a hot flush threatens to ignite you. This also entails trying not to draw unwelcome attention to yourself, and being able to surreptitiously put them all back on later when you realise you are cold. It's entirely possible that this process may have to be repeated multiple times during the course of one meeting. It makes it difficult to maintain a cool professional demeanour. I do wonder what the workplace would be like if men encountered these biological storms.

The conversations showed me that the core component seems to be to find a way of being *centred*, to use Liberty's earlier term. Some of the women have found approaches that have helped them do that – having colour analysis for instance.

I am finding that my reflections during and following the conversations have led me to relax a little so that I can embrace the issue rather than continuing to try to avoid it. I've bought a full length mirror for the first time. I clearly seem to be rather slow on the uptake, but I've realised it is a good idea to know what you've already got in the wardrobe. Another good idea is to take some time to try on what you already own, in front of the aforementioned mirror. Maybe ask for honest (and if you're lucky, supportive) second opinions if you can find a willing someone (it may be worth looking beyond your family on this one).

I've also had the revelation (this might be obvious to other women) that it's an on-going issue. I don't have to find my own elusive style in one attempt. Indeed, why would I expect it to stay the same for the rest of my days? I can buy one or two things now and one or two things next year or season. I can play with styles and colours. With help from my long-suffering hairdresser, I know that I am 'cool winter' in terms of the colour part of the equation. Searching for images on the internet with that in mind brings up loads of inviting ideas. It suddenly looks fun.

It all adds up to a new strategy for me. I am making fewer clothes decisions but they are considered ones rather than my habitual approach of making a greater number of snap ones. I feel as if the stakes have been lowered. It's a start. Although it's yet to be given a thorough Scottish autumn test.

Extreme measures

I've met people who have done Botox and when you get close it's horrible, you can see all the puffiness. I couldn't do surgical, I just couldn't.
—Marie

I look at my jowls and my droopy chin and I think oh dear. But you know what? That's who I am. I've had enough surgery that I've needed to have not to choose surgery to end up with pouty lips or whatever.
—Helen

I am interested in how we construct our norms. Previous generations have thought it normal (and therefore attractive and desirable) for women to be very curvy or very thin, very white or very brown. Women have been disabled by almost every intervention imaginable: constricted waists, bound feet, toxic make-up, dangerous diets, and crippling fashions. It's not all history either.

Cosmetic surgery or interventions like Botox are not procedures I am familiar with beyond a cursory glance at magazines. I'm not drawn to such approaches to deal with ageing, and neither were the women I spoke to. It's not a field I know much about and as far as I am aware, none of my close friends have gone down this route.

I am not in a position to judge any of these practices in and of themselves, but I am interested in how what seems like an extreme measure to one generation becomes normal to another. Attitudes to hair removal and women's proportions over the years demonstrate this process very clearly.

I suspect that this progression of norms is speeding up and affecting a greater number of people in the internet age. The development of new technology means more beauty procedures are more readily available, and global media enables us to compare ourselves with other women far more than ever before.

I come back to my underlying thoughts about ageing. No amount of intervention is going to prevent us from getting older. Learning to live with that thought isn't easy especially in an environment where a greater number of us are probably more judgemental about appearance than at any other time in history. This can lead us to feel that we have no choice but to go down ever more extreme routes to try to stop or turn back the clock. And from what I can see, men (especially young men) are being drawn into this futile quest in greater numbers too.

I don't want to go there. The conversations did nothing to change my mind on that.

Perspective and dining tables

It's who I am inside that matters. And the people that matter are the ones that can see inside me. The outward appearance is far less important. I'm not saying that I don't want to look nice but it's not important.
—Simran

I think there is too much emphasis on what you look like and looking young. I suppose nobody wants to look really old and wrinkled but it's inevitable. Eventually, if you live long enough, you're going to have wrinkles, and I think that's to be accepted. Look beyond it.
—Pat

From childhood onwards, I have loved old wooden tables. I'll stare at them, and hope I can touch them, in any kitchen or dining room of any stately home or museum we've visited. Even better are those in modest homes that have survived.

Dented, scratched, polished and waxed, they may have been cherished or taken for granted for centuries. They evoke the past and the present, and are a tangible connection with history: the conversations, laughter, arguments, food, friendships, disasters and triumphs in any family in any age. To my mind, they get more beautiful with age as these significant pieces of furniture develop a distinctive patina.

Listening to the conversations, it seems to me that we all develop our own, human version of this patina over the decades. It's an idea that I find comforting.

This patina shows us our life story. Our eventual appearance shows what our lives have been about. The wrinkles and lines reflect habitual expressions. The scars reflect events. The quality of our skin, muscles, hair and teeth reflects both our genetic lot in life as well as what kind of lifestyle we have led. It is our life, laid bare.

The loveliest ancient tables are the ones that have been cared for as well as being used. Countless layers of nourishing beeswax have been applied by countless generations. Many elbows have worn dips in the wood. Fabric and fingers have smoothed the surface. Heat, cutlery, accidents and carelessness – life – have made scars.

Cosmetic surgery and harsh chemical treatments seem akin to taking a plane or bottle of acid to a table to try to restore its original surface. There may be times when that is the best thing to do, but more often than not I would guess it risks doing more harm than good. And very often the seasoned surface is more attractive than the original one anyway.

From the conversations, appearance seems both more and less important to me than I thought it was. It feels unexpectedly alright to take some care over it without feeling guiltily vain, or stumbling around in ignorance. But by the same token, it feels right to accept that there is much about it that cannot be controlled or changed. Gently letting it be is often the most liberating way forward.

How we balance energy, money and time spent on appearance with the actual business of living is, I feel, a very personal decision. It takes some trial and error to get a comfortable equilibrium.

I believe that the patina that results from a good balance can be every bit as beautiful as youth. It's just different. (And yes – I did buy the moisturiser with the loyalty points).

WHAT MATTERS

- Nurturing vitality and well-being – it shows in your appearance
- Asking for help and supportive feedback
- Noticing and challenging assumptions that link age and appearance
- Recognising and accepting what you can't change
- Playing with what you can change – colours and style in particular

WHAT DOESN'T

- Anti-ageing
- Rules about what older women should look like
- The colour of your hair – it's up to you. Enjoy.
- Searching for a forever style
- Having the same attitude to appearance every day

CHAPTER 3

WEDDED (OR UNWEDDED) BLISS

Decisions, decisions – a sense of us – a sense of me –
negotiation – the long view – love, sex and romance –
what matters – what doesn't

Staying with the theme of dining tables for a moment – for the last time – my parents have a dining table that is not any shape that I know the name of. My dad made it. The story goes that when they set up house, one of them wanted a rectangular table and one an oval one.

So they compromised. It is a kind of blown up rectangle. It has corners, and also curved sides. It has served well for fifty years of marriage and continues to do so.

I have never been able to decide if I see this as a deeply loving symbol of marriage or a result of unresolved differences. Of course, it doesn't much matter what I think.

Long term relationships, whether sealed with marriage or not, are one of the biggest mysteries of life. None of us can ever know quite what it's like to be in someone else's marriage or relationship. Most of us only see one or two examples from close quarters as we grow up and it's usually from a very vested interest perspective.

It can lead us to copy those patterns, unwittingly or not, or to go out of our way to do something completely different.

For most of us, our expectations, roles and duties are not set as clearly by state, religion and tradition as they once would have been. This has been liberating for many, with a welcome chance to change or escape what they may have had to endure, in past decades. Along with choices though, come decisions.

Decisions, decisions...

My mother encouraged me to get out and have a life. It was based on her own regret about being drawn into something without being herself.
—Helen

I decided I had to make it work. This was my path. It was hard, but there have been some really good bits to it.
—Simran

I was never bothered about marriage. I couldn't tell you what year we got married. We did it because I had so little pension.
—Lesley

The days when most women's expectations were limited to simply growing up, getting married and having children were disappearing fast by the time my women were reaching adulthood. Even though it may still have raised eyebrows not to get married, it was no longer the only route forward. In general, marriage no longer precluded having a job or career for these women, particularly the younger women in my group.

This opened opportunities for unprecedented levels of decision making. I was slightly surprised at first by the firm pragmatism that accompanied some of the decisions about marriage. As I listened, I was increasingly impressed by it. It didn't mean that there was a lack of love or romance, but there was a clear appreciation of the practical implications of marriage for them. They all struck me – whether married for a long time or more than once, widowed or not married at all – to have their feet firmly on the ground. The conversations recognised the advantages and disadvantages of being married. Hearing what it has really been like for these women was refreshing.

Some have had very long and successful marriages which seemed characterised by very honest recognition of the irritations, against an overall backdrop of a highly supportive partnership. The work and commitment involved in developing such a partnership was clear.

For these women and especially for my generation and women younger than me, there are choices open to us about whether to live with someone, whether to marry them and whether to stay with them, which were largely unheard of prior to the middle of the twentieth century. These decisions are not easy ones. None of us can predict how things will turn out, whatever we decide. Not all of us get to decide either, if the person we would like to be with doesn't want to stay with us.

What I learned from the conversations was often about how women (and their husbands) went about working at their relationships. It certainly didn't seem for any of them to be a simple case of meeting 'The One' and living happily ever after.

The circumstances and spark between them when they met and decided to be together really was just the beginning for the marriages described. Since then, over decades for some of them, it has been something of a white-water experience of highs, lows and calm stretches. Interestingly, and importantly, it has also involved some deep introspection for many of these women, in understanding and accepting *themselves* at different stages of their life as well as how they relate to their husbands or partners. It confirmed what I've gradually become aware of over the years. It is difficult to be loving and present for someone else if you are struggling to be that with yourself.

It's an on-going process. These women reflected on how life events had strengthened or threatened their marriages. They reflected on what they had gained from relationships that may not have worked out in the long term. A process of continual adjustment went on, knowingly or not. Decisions to stay, or go, cropped up at intervals for some. For me, married for the second time, it was riveting to listen to.

A sense of us

Many things can be terrifying on your own but if you have company, it's an adventure. Having company, and having somebody to help restore your sense of proportion, are important. Not everyone knows how to help the other person do that.
—Nicole

I think friendship in marriage is very important.
—Pat

We were not in the same orbit enough. It was part of the downfall of our marriage. We were like two tops spinning, at huge speed and never stopped.
—Jane

When I was about twenty, one of my friends returned from his older sister's wedding. It provoked a heated conversation amongst a group of us about what coupledom meant. I clearly recall the friend whose sister it was vowing never to say 'we like this kind of music' or 'we don't like this kind of food' (I can't remember if the unsuspecting sister was being accused of such a crime). His views chimed with my lifelong horror of 'his and hers' matching coats or jumpers.

Long term relationships seem to be an undertaking in balancing 'we' versus 'I'. What is comfortable for one couple is anathema to another. But what the conversations brought out was how the 'we' *and* 'I' are both important.

I was particularly struck by the comments about companionship. Shortly after my separation from my first husband, there were record floods in our area and also industrial action that threatened fuel supplies (I don't think these were a result of our separation, I hasten to add). My children were too young to understand what was going on, and in any case I didn't want them to be alarmed. But watching the evening news on my own left no opportunity to remark or discuss. I was mildly concerned about where events were heading but had nowhere to go with those worries. I had opinions I wanted to express. I wanted to gasp or rant at the images on the television in unison with someone else. I missed simple companionship.

It is equivalent to wearing your slippers. It can sound unromantic, dull and predictable. But for the long term, in many of the conversations, this was a key ingredient for a happy marriage. And I for one, just love putting my slippers on. It doesn't mean you have to wear them all the time.

Companionship does depend on being together for enough of the time to build up a stock of shared experiences and habits.

Several of the conversations reflected, either from first-hand experience or from observation of friends and acquaintances, that some couples ended up inhabiting different worlds because there weren't enough habitual, vanilla flavoured, companionable hours. When that happened it seemed to create the opportunity for something – or someone – else to enter the marriage and often this was a factor in the demise of the relationship.

How many hours are to be spent in companionable silence or inane repetition of opinions is, I suspect, not easily advised. It remains one of the mysteries of what actually happens behind our friends' and families' front doors when we're not there to witness or join in. Some element of it seems important though.

A further aspect of companionship is the sense of 'being in it together'. As Nicole put it, having someone to help you regain your perspective when you feel frightened or tired or stressed is valuable. She also recognises that sometimes partners are unable to do that, particularly if one person is compellingly anxious. It's for this reason that most of us need other people beyond our own relationship as well.

This struck home for me. It was a big factor from my perspective in what went wrong in my first marriage. We both felt tired, frightened and stressed at times (as does everyone) and when this became a prolonged state of mind for either one of us, we would tend to drag the other one into that quagmire. When a difficult pregnancy and parenthood came along, on top of some years of uncertainty about career direction and demanding jobs, this was an all too common scenario for us. We did our best to cope with what were relatively normal conditions for many families, but we could both be compellingly anxious in our own ways.

It's not a phrase I'd heard before but I recognised it in what I've observed in my parents at times as well as in myself and others. It is beyond just feeling anxious – it is about trying to convince the other person that they should be anxious too. Somehow if they're not, we don't think they realise the full import of what is going on. When I'm in full tilt worry mode, I can see that's what I do (*Can't you see the disaster ahead? Why aren't you taking this as seriously as I am? You can't know it will be ok. What are we going to do? We're doomed...*). I argue forcefully and eloquently with their calming reassurances. I try to persuade them to see the situation from my point of view. He may not agree, but I think my first husband also did that at that time. We tended to keep pulling each other into the quicksand.

But the bonding that *can* result from dealing with challenging situations together is not to be underestimated. The conversations left the impression that the shared reminiscences resulting from weathering various storms together put a different spin on difficult circumstances. The events themselves might have been stressful and testing. There's no guarantee but they can lead to an increased team spirit, with a good dose of humour in hindsight, even if the events themselves were far from funny. Although we are no longer married, my first husband and I have managed to form a new kind of team-work as parents over the years.

My second husband and I have a different dynamic. We've both learned a lot over the years, including, for me, how to manage anxiety more successfully. We're older. We both get stressed and tired at times but try not to convince the other one to do the same.

I'm happy to say that this doesn't mean we have to have matching team coats.

A sense of me

*I'm lucky that my husband has always let me be who I am,
and encouraged me to be. We'd never have been able to survive
otherwise.*
—Val

Learn to listen. Give each other space.
—Christine

*It's about enabling each of us to reach our potential. It's a
mindset. It's not about asking permission.*
—Madeline

All of the women I spoke to wanted – and needed – space to be
themselves. In fact, I would say that this was the most prized
aspect of marriage that they talked about. They did not want
to merge into a 'we' that did everything together, or shared all
interests or opinions. Most echoed the student conversation my
friend initiated all those years ago.

There were parts of their lives that their husbands could
probably never truly understand (and I would guess that this is
true for men too). Working out how to be heard, and how to
develop as a person in your own right, as well as how to operate
as one half of a partnership, is an almighty challenge. It has not
been uncommon for big jolts to have been necessary for that
to happen. Electric shocks have been applied to some of these
relationships from time to time. Not all of them survived such
extreme measures.

I particularly identified with women who spoke about
their need for time and space for their creative work. Some

write, some paint and draw, some are musicians. They all love learning. None of this is possible without somewhere to do it and time alone to immerse yourself in it. It is hard to overstate how important this was in the lives of the women I listened to, especially as they reached their fifties and beyond.

I find it immensely sad when people have suppressed their own personalities or interests in order to fit in with the marriage and family life they are in, or a perceived ideal. This used to be common for women (and maybe more men than we might think). It doesn't have to be that way now even though pressures still clearly exist that lead to very real imbalances in relationships of all sorts.

All long term relationships have to find their own balance between 'we' and 'me'. Each one will be unique and I think of it as the fingerprint of the marriage. There are no rules about what that balance should be, but most of the women I listened to were clear that finding a balance that worked was crucial. The balance may also change over the years and need re-negotiating. I think it is easy to forget that.

Negotiation

We both said, if this isn't going to work, I'm opting out. It was scary. But I thought, wow, even though I love this guy, I'm not going to get into another relationship that's going to hurt me.
—Madeline

The ground rules were laid down a very long time ago. When something came up that was an issue I stood my ground. I said,

*I won't neglect the family but I have to do this. I think some
people don't do that in their marriages.*
—Tanje

*I left the family home for about nine months. It felt very
important to re-negotiate the relationship. It wasn't about
blaming him, but about examining what we had both allowed
to happen.*
—Anne

Compromise, which led to the unique construction of my
parents' table, was a word that frequently came up in relation to
marriage on the occasions my parents spoke about such things.
I was never quite comfortable with the concept. As a relatively
accommodating teenager, it seemed to me to run a dangerous
risk of one or both parties *being compromised*. This seemed
(and still does) to be an entirely different thing from actively
reaching agreement from two viewpoints.

Active compromise in terms of reaching so called win-
win outcomes, in any situation, is hard work. It requires
assertiveness, compassion and creativity. It is not purely
about fairness, which might lead to a lose-lose outcome – one
that is fair but it doesn't meet anyone's needs. And it is very
different from one party reluctantly agreeing with the other's
wishes and coming away with a corrosive resentment which
is gradually nursed into boiling anger over the ensuing weeks
and years.

In my own blended family situation (we are both married
for the second time, and both bring children with us), it is all
too easy for our marriage to get squashed whilst we pass each
other like ships in the night. The daily normal turmoil of lifts,

meals, work, school, exams, hobbies, extended family and, on occasion, sheer exhaustion, can be a challenge.

For me, the conversations have been like opening a door for a while on this commonplace and often secretive institution. What has struck me most is that there is nothing rose-tinted about it. Successful long term relationships are hewn out of granite and oak, using chisels and saws. As the quote goes, any more than ageing itself, it is not an undertaking for sissies.

It is sleeves-rolled-up team work. It's about how to reconcile one view against another. It's about how to harness the complementary elements rather than allowing them to be rage-inducing differences. It's about not losing anyone's identity.

Negotiations may indeed result in compromise. We can't have our own way all the time if we share our lives with other people. But not all decisions can result in a half-way house even if we do have advanced carpentry skills.

Sometimes, as individuals, we need both to understand what our position is and step up to argue our case. Neither of those things is necessarily easy, especially to do it in a way that doesn't hurt anyone unnecessarily. I personally don't find it easy at all. It can be much more tempting to avoid possible confrontation.

What has been helpful for me from the conversations is realising that wrestling with differences is core to any long term relationship – so it's normal – as well as recognising that it takes considerable energy, courage and patience to engage in such negotiations. Surprisingly, I find this reassuring.

Rather than trying to avoid such moments, perhaps it's healthier to welcome them. Choosing what to negotiate over and what to let go of is part of this. The conversations have made me more aware of that choice.

When I can feel myself getting angry with my husband, I don't like it. My reflex reaction is to swing wildly between assuming that it must be me to blame, and an angrily defensive stance that it must be his fault. It's only later that I might remember that apportioning blame won't get us anywhere. Either way, my automatic stance is one of avoidance. Unless I remember to do otherwise (and I am getting better at this), I tend not to communicate my feelings in a direct way but to try to rise above it, turn the other cheek, ignore it or assume I'm making a mountain out of a molehill. And then secretly worry that it is indeed a mountain.

Although it doesn't happen very often, when I am angry, I either withdraw in quiet fury or explode in shaky rage. Or both, which is never pretty. It all leaves my equilibrium in tatters.

The anger is usually triggered by some commonplace disagreement. Sometimes it's about more fundamental differences. Parenting in a step family isn't always the easiest thing in the world either. There is nothing exceptional about any of this. It must be repeated in millions of other households.

What the conversations have helped me to do is to shift my perception. Anger about differences is not a sign of some feared extreme: that our marriage is broken, or that I'm intolerant, or that he's impossible. It is a call to action. A call to the negotiating table – whatever shape it is.

The long view

You look back and you think you could have divorced ninety times. Lots of people did. I'm glad we didn't.
—Lesley

I respect his profession and he respects mine. That's the core. It's a knot that ties us.
—Liberty

I could not have done what I've done without my ex-husband. We were married for 21 years and we're still great friends.
—Jane

I was warmed by the philosophical nature of the reflections on long term relationships and marriage that were expressed in the majority of the conversations. Even when those marriages had ended or were extremely difficult, there was still a widespread appreciation about the part their relationships had played in each of these women's lives.

It was also clear that many relationships are complicated. Over many years and with such history, expectation and experience, how could they not be? These women are old enough to be able to see the ebb and flow as they look back and I find that reassuring when I get caught in the occasionally tense moments that can occur at our stage of life. Things are rarely black or white. It takes some perspective to see that.

Another unexpected perspective emerged in several conversations where the women revealed that they feel they work well as a couple when they are on holiday. This is definitely the case for me and my husband, particularly the holidays we have managed to carve out for just the two of us. In recent years, for us, this has best manifested itself in our on-going project to walk, in stages, the South West Coast path, which runs for 630 miles around the coast from Somerset to Dorset. We've walked about half of it so far.

It usually does wonders for us in re-connecting. Sometimes we talk whilst walking, sometimes we don't. We share a great enthusiasm for that part of the country and the quirky little bits of history and geography we pick up on the way. We are like-minded when it comes to meals and breaks.

Until the conversations, I tended to regard this as exceptional time, a luxury indulgence which wasn't somehow 'real life'. I felt that our marriage should be more accurately measured by how we were on a wet, cold February evening after long days at work, looming deadlines, multiple agendas from the children, juggling meals, and perhaps with a few errands or chores to do. The kind of evening that would typically be rounded off by falling asleep on the sofa whilst struggling to follow some plot-heavy drama serial.

The conversations have shed a different light on this for me. Perhaps the holiday time *is* real and the more trying times are a reflection of the phase we're in. Maybe each is just as real as the other. Life is one phase after another. The conversations would suggest that happiness may lie in accepting that.

Holidays give us the moments where we can re-ignite shared interests and companionship, and have adventures. They are the times when we are not torn in many directions and are not too tired to form a sentence. They lay down the shared memories that help to preserve our sanity and happiness in older age. From this perspective, holidays are not a luxury – though of course budgets may well vary dramatically over different phases – but essential glue to a long term relationship. I don't think they even have to be conventionally successful holidays. Some of the most disastrous breaks provide stories for life.

Perhaps the high days and holidays are the links between phases and challenges. The stitches in time. The punctuation.

I doubt it matters at all what kind of holiday. I have known people go on silent retreats together or triathlon training camps, and everything in between. That aspect will be yet another negotiation. It seems to be one worth having.

Love, sex and romance

I have a wonderful, caring, loving, thoughtful, patient, generous, supportive husband.
—Tanje

We've had loads of laughs. We've been lucky.
—Val

I'm lucky I suppose. I've had a happy marriage. It's quite unusual these days for people to stay together for 52 years.
—Pat

It was only when I came to write up the conversations that I realised the words 'love', 'sex' and 'romance' came up infrequently in response to my question about what matters and what doesn't about marriage and long term relationships.

There may well be an element of British reserve behind that, from both me and some of the women (not all of them are British though). These were already intimate conversations. I felt that asking specifically about sex risked being a distraction from some of the themes I have explored (I may have missed a marketing trick though).

As I reflected afterwards, I think there is something else going on, beyond the reserve. In a word association exercise, many of us would respond with terms such as love, sex and romance when given the word 'marriage'. But historically, marrying for love (or lust) is a relatively modern concept, and is not the norm in all cultures. I have no doubt that most of the marriages I heard about are loving, or have been at some stages, and most began with the couple falling in love. I find it moving to hear some of the women talk in such warmly positive terms about their relationships, and this is something to be rightly celebrated.

But we are fed very idealistic notions through stories, magazines and films. Back in the real world, love in the long term is complex. It is not a film script or escapist novel. The words the women used to describe their relationships are much more varied, grounded and meaningful. They resonate with my own mixed experience.

I find it enormously heartening. Marriage can be a something of a bumpy road, even when it is judged to be a success. How love and passion translate into years of living together isn't always obvious. What counts as loving and romantic in the long term may not be demonstrative or sentimental in a Hollywood sense. It may be about supporting the other person to develop their own interests, or it may lie in remembering to put the bin out. It may be about knowing when to provide a cup of tea without asking or it may be about when and how to argue. It may be about wild abandoned sex or it may be about a hug when you get home. The details don't seem to matter that much. It's the overall picture that does.

WHAT MATTERS

- Warm realism in the long term
- Friendship in marriage
- Holidays
- The courage to negotiate

WHAT DOESN'T

- Other people's expectations and imagined norms
- Artificial or commercial notions of love and romance
- The details of what works for you – all that matters is that it works
- Marriage at all costs – especially if it means suppressing your personality or interests

CHAPTER 4

GIRLS' OWN ADVENTURES

Breaking out of perfectionism – the intrepid
traveller – making a difference – adventures in
creativity – memories – encouragement and equipment –
what matters – what doesn't

The sea battered the cliff far below us on our left. The path narrowed at the same time as the wind increased. The well maintained barbed wire fence on our right was festooned with important signs that made it clear no one was to cross over into the field beyond. I was following my (then) husband. He had our baby daughter in a back pack. She was enjoying herself, having a great view over the sea and Scottish countryside. She gurgled and waved her arms around.

I could feel fearful sweat building as I started to have all too clear visions of me or him missing our footing and plunging to the foaming surf and rocks below us. I kept up a calming sing song refrain to myself, *it'll be ok, it'll be ok.* And then I spotted a party walking towards us. The path was only wide enough for single file anyway. *How* were we going to pass each other? Suddenly, I couldn't take another step. I unwisely vaulted – well, sort of scrambled – over the ferocious fence, ripping my clothes (and legs) in the process. I hauled the baby carrier, still complete with cheerful baby, into the field. I simply could not hold my nerve any longer.

The rest of the walk was uneventful. The baby is now nearly eighteen.

I have never thought of myself as an adventurous person. I am not widely travelled, I didn't strike out on a gap year (still waiting), and I've always been pretty good at crossing imaginary bridges in advance. I can usually see potential dangers and setbacks in unhelpfully clear detail. I don't enjoy the feeling of fear.

Since having children, my sense of physical danger has intensified – I suspect it comes with the territory. This, combined with not great balance and eyesight, and a propensity to bang my head on anything possible, has led to some legendary moments amongst my friends. They discovered that I meant it when I said I was unlikely to be good at ice-skating, or abseiling.

Having said all that, I do know what it feels like to have a quiet core of determination – some might call it bloody mindedness – and I have often set out at least on psychological adventures if not physical ones. I headed off to university, without knowing anyone else when I got there. I changed career, set up a business, had children, separated from my first husband, started writing. I found whatever was needed to cope with these events because it actually felt as if I had no choice at all. If I was to survive with myself intact I *needed* to do these things.

Where I've been much more cautious is when things have felt more optional. Actions that might seem like more conventional challenges – physical derring-do, or travelling – have not been high on my agenda. There have been some notable exceptions, such as the trip to Cuba, but I don't undertake these things lightly. It was outside of my comfort zone. I was keen to hear how to manage the siren call that the comfort zone emits.

Breaking out of perfectionism

The fear of failure is a terrible thing. One of my oldest friends won't do anything that isn't already perfect. It really worries her to risk it so she doesn't engage in things.
—Rose

Another beauty of getting older is that it's lovely to fail. There is no failure, it's feedback. When you're younger that failure is a big thing.
—Simran

As we get older, it becomes increasingly possible to live out our days in our comfort zone if we so wish. We develop strategies that may shield us from fear by avoiding uncomfortable situations. Sometimes this may be the best thing to do. Most of us appreciate a level of safety in our lives.

But never venturing out of our comfort zone is likely to leave us in a state of complacency. We may be bored and fearful underneath the comfort. The safety it offers is an illusion as it can never protect us from unforeseen events. Whilst we're there, we're not usually learning a lot about ourselves or other people. By not risking new experiences, the comfort zone can slowly turn into a prison. It has a tendency to become slightly smaller as the years pass.

We are all different. One woman's terrifying escapade is another's walk in the park. How we define the boundaries around our comfort zones will vary from person to person. What seems important, and was a theme throughout the conversations, is to understand when it is fear rather than desire that is keeping us in our own secure area. This does not mean that we should all be out there taming tigers every day of our lives. It is not saying we cannot be content with our lifestyles and choices. It is about understanding ourselves well enough to know when we are being held back by fear of failure or habitually playing it safe.

I think it is a rare person who genuinely doesn't fear failure in any sphere. No one proposed in the conversations that we should try to overcome all of it. I would fear failure as a lion (or tiger) tamer and I'm happy to live with that. I enjoy those times when I know what I'm doing and I'm relaxed doing it.

However, many of us (and I include myself here) take on a perfectionist mindset throughout our childhood and young adulthood almost by osmosis it seems. Perhaps the way we are judged through the education system and then in a wider sense through the media and cultural norms means that it's difficult to avoid altogether. There is nothing wrong with striving to do something well. But there can be problems when the goal of perfection stops us doing things that we don't think we will be good at immediately, or where the outcome is uncertain.

It came up many times in the conversations that this is an unhelpful mindset. It limits our experiences and can keep us locked into a place we reached many years ago. It can be rejuvenating to surprise ourselves. It doesn't matter what with – it could be learning to swim, or writing a poem, or climbing the Himalayas or having an unexpected conversation with an old friend. Just don't expect perfection.

The intrepid traveller

My son-in-law said, 'I reckon you could climb Mont Blanc.'
And I said, 'Don't be so stupid'. But I did. I raised £10,000 for
the oesophageal patients' association. I was 69.
—Kitty

My friend was widowed too, about twenty years ago. We
started going round Europe and then went to India, China – by
way of Uzbekistan.
—Rose

I went off backpacking for four and half months round the
world. I was 58.
—Linda

Travelling is a sure fire way of inviting some adventure into our lives. I was excited by some of the tales I heard. What especially encouraged me was that age did not appear to be the limitation that I had perhaps expected.

To a degree, health will be a restriction. However, hearing about the Mont Blanc climb which Kitty did *after* surviving cancer, I was forced to wonder how much we limit ourselves by what we *think* we're capable of rather than absolutes. I suspect the same applies to perceived financial limitations too. There are ways and means if you want to do something enough.

The conversations left me with a sense that adventurous travelling is attainable for older women. Indeed, it may not be until later life that the opportunity arises. The women quoted above undertook these ventures after serious illness, bereavement or divorce, and after their children were well into adulthood. These were valuable lessons that it's not over till it's over.

What I have understood from the conversations is that being outward facing is very important as we get older. This applies in many ways. It needs active maintenance, and is not something to take for granted.

Do we look inward, trying to preserve things as they are, and turning our backs on new experiences? Or do we keep the gate open as we look over the comfort zone fence to see what's going on elsewhere? Both take energy. Both involve risk whether we perceive it as such or not.

Travelling is not the only way of challenging ourselves to look outward, but it is a very tangible way of doing that. It can take many forms and result in a myriad of different experiences. It doesn't necessarily have to be far flung or involve backpacks. It's more to do with curiosity than mileage.

I'm pleased to feel that there are still numerous possibilities out there even though I am no longer in my twenties. I can't know what the coming decades hold in terms of opportunities to travel – but I have learnt that my age shouldn't be the defining limitation.

Making a difference

Did I tell you that I'm standing for the County Council next year?
—Anne

I got involved in a project in Moldova training therapists and carers for three months. I needed to do something by myself,

without my husband. It was very hard but it helped me a lot
with my confidence.
—Christine

We were given two weeks to train boy soldiers in the Sudan.
The Commandant positioned us as subordinates by the way he
introduced us. He told the boys they were not to speak unless
we spoke to them to or they would go back to being soldiers.
We couldn't get them to shift from that position.
—Madeline

Some of the adventures that I heard about were motivated by
an urge to make a difference in some way. They involved the
women using their existing experience and expertise in a new
field or environment. Some were at home, others abroad.

There are many examples of the women going well beyond
their comfort zone, and I reflected that an extra element of
courage seemed to come from the beliefs behind these decisions.
In some cases, this is religious faith. In others, it is political
conviction or a passion to address a social issue. It allows
adventure to be based on something bigger than the individual.
It enabled the women to volunteer or commit to actions that
they may not have done otherwise.

I found their stories motivating and awe-inspiring. Women –
of all ages – are embracing extremely challenging situations and
often improving people's lives as a result. They are using these
experiences to communicate with the wider world and to explore
the underlying concerns that they encounter. They have valuable
experience to bring to the projects and roles that they take on.

They are challenging themselves and the people they meet
to step up, without being sure that they will be successful. They

are engaging politically and socially despite some considerable barriers. They are doing it by focusing on other people's needs rather than their own. It's another route to adventure.

Adventures in creativity

I started writing when I was about 55. My husband said, don't you find it too revealing? I write more easily now I'm on my own. I'm not worried about revealing things. What the hell!
—Rose

Nobody has any demands on my art work but me. I sink or swim because of my decisions.
—Val

Creativity involves risk. It can lead to big adventures without even leaving the house. Age is not a limitation.

The richness of experience that being creative has brought many of the women I listened to was striking. Having a creative outlet is a gift that goes on giving. There are few circumstances that prevent us from engaging at some level and in some way. There is usually some way of incorporating it into day to day existence. History is full of examples of people who have managed to do that even in the face of severe disability, illness or other dire situations.

From what I heard, the biggest barrier is the small internal voice that tells us we're not creative. It can become a firmly held belief which inhibits our attempts to have a go at any kind of creative endeavour.

I have always enjoyed writing but it wasn't until a few years ago that I started to take the brakes off. Two things helped me to do that. One is the on-line annual novel writing exercise that takes place in November (www.nanowrimo.org). The other was a creative writing course I undertook with the Open University. Until then, I had written small amounts in a secretive way, feeling overly self-conscious even when I was the only person in the room. Looking back, that seems ridiculous. But I remember being paralysed by the empty screen or page. The inner editor tore every sentence to shreds before I could even get it written down.

It took some practice simply to write without judging. But I am well aware now that there is no other way. Nothing appears on the page fully formed. Much has to be created in order to later be discarded or replaced. The idea that eventually works is rarely the first one. This is true in every art or craft form as far as I'm aware.

It's only since I learnt just to write, then edit my words later, that I feel more comfortable calling myself creative. It's invigorating. It allows me to play with ideas and words. It is core to progress in every field that people engage in, as far as I can see.

Silencing the inner critic feels both liberating and scary. It is also essential, certainly in the early stages of developing an idea or following a creative urge. It is revealing. We might see ourselves in a new way. Others might see us differently if we show them what we're doing. It's impossible to commit yourself to a creative activity without running that risk.

It means we learn things about ourselves and each other. We might start to see fresh meaning in familiar things or explore unfamiliar aspects of ourselves. It can be every bit as exhilarating and uncomfortable as physical adventure. And from listening to the conversations, the good news I heard is that it's hardly ever too late to start.

Memories

As an adult looking back at some of the things I did, I think, oh no....but actually I'm glad I did them. Going off with the National Youth Theatre, living in London, coping, being scared witless. It was fun.
—Helen

I got up when I wanted, I went to bed when I wanted, I ate when I wanted, I didn't eat if I didn't want, I learnt to read a map, I travelled on local transport – and I had the most amazing time.
—Linda

What was clear from many of the conversations was how much the women had gained from building a stock of vibrant memories. These come from all areas of their lives of course, but the particularly colourful tales often came from the adventures. They came from decisions to be brave, and from times when they have taken risks. Listening to them, their voices and faces lit up as they recounted exciting times. It was energising to listen to.

These undertakings have given them tales to tell afterwards, and an air of confidence as they look back at what they achieved or experienced. The value of adventure seems to be not only in the events themselves but in their aftermath.

Perhaps this has always been part of the allure of adventurous journeys. Telling stories later by the safety of your fireside has a joy of its own. The anecdotes, the memories and the way in which these things have altered the women I spoke to have stayed with me. The things they learned about themselves and the shift in outlook that occurred, have helped them to transcend their familiar roles as wives or mothers, colleagues and friends.

Reminiscing can be a comforting and happy activity at any age. The half-forgotten scent of good memories can waft into consciousness in a way that feels soothing, calming, cheering. I'm aware of this when we get old photo albums out. The effect is the same on my children as it is on the older members of the family. Whatever our current challenges are, we remember the good times. The funny times. The scary times that we survived. Even the times of huge family rows or upset have sunk into collective memory with a wry smile in our family.

As a child myself (and still today), I loved it when my parents' generation started recalling favourite stories from their youth. These probably somewhat tall tales were familiar to all of us (even if the events themselves were from before our time). We would still end up in helpless laughter once again as the bizarre arrangements around my great-aunt's funeral or the hilarious moments in my father and uncle's spell in a tuberculosis sanatorium were recalled. (Really. I was brought up on black humour).

I have come away from the conversations reminded of how valuable the memories formed by adventures can be, to warm us later like a good bottle of aged spirit. A nip now and then can do a world of good.

Encouragement and equipment

I was fifty when I started my degree. I remember asking one of the tutors whether she thought that I could do it. When I came out of her office, I felt literally as though I was walking on air. Doing the degree was down to her encouragement.
—Margaret

My friend said, 'I've always wanted to climb Mont Blanc. I'll be seventy-five next year. We'll do it together and I'll train you.'
—Kitty

Several of the conversations revealed turning points, when other people had been instrumental in providing just the right amount of encouragement at the right moment. Most of us need it.

It's not always our nearest and dearest that are first to offer it. If we decide to undertake some adventure, necessarily involving some risk, it can feel threatening to our family or friends. They might be worried about our safety or about what impact our actions might have on their relationship with us. These understandable reactions can act as a barrier, holding us back.

The conversations did not make me think it was necessarily good to dismiss close friends' and family's possible objections to our ideas. We are wise to take them into account. But we may well need to seek out other opinions too, from a less invested perspective. I could see how helpful that had been for many of the women I listened to.

I also saw how beneficial it had been for women to prepare themselves well for adventure. Whatever form of exploit, it was common to seek support and to learn from experienced teachers and guides, who were sometimes decades younger than the women themselves. Whilst risk is inherent, none of these women struck me as reckless. They had worked hard at being fit enough for physical challenge. They had booked ahead for more hazardous parts of their travels. They had sought mentorship or training for skills they might need. They asked for help when necessary.

Excitement and fear are closely related emotions and one can tip into the other in an instant. It's that fiery mix that tells us when we are outside of our comfort zone. There can be a big temptation to calm ourselves by retreating – which is sometimes the best thing to do. But there are other times when we ultimately benefit by staying with the adrenaline rush to see what might lie beyond. Other people can help us hold our nerve.

It's ironic that inhabiting the centre of a shrinking comfort zone is, it seems, a potentially very risky way to age. Despite appearances, it can be isolating, and permeated with fear. It is worth remembering.

WHAT MATTERS

- Facing outward
- Seeking the right kind of encouragement
- Preparing to a realistic level, mentally and physically
- Recognising when it is fear, not choice, that holds us back
- Cherishing memories

WHAT DOESN'T

- The nature of the adventure
- Being perfect
- Trying to cross all potential bridges in advance
- Being too trusting of our perception of risk – we're often wrong
- Feeling fear – it comes with the territory

CHAPTER 5

MOTHERHOOD

The umbilical yank – an inexact science – independence and identity – qué será será – all or nothing – what matters – what doesn't

....

I became a mother at 31, and had my second child two years later. They are both girls. My second husband's son is the same age as my eldest daughter. Although my stepson is very much part of our family, he has never lived full-time with us and visits less frequently as his teens have progressed. For me, motherhood and step-motherhood have been different experiences. I am focusing on motherhood in this chapter.

In my case, turning 50 is inextricably linked with the emerging adulthood of the children. One of my daughters reaches 18 when I am 49, the other when I am 51. There seem to be rather closer similarities between adolescence and menopause than I was expecting. In some ways all three of us are locked into an identity struggle. Part of that is a private experience; part of it is about the dynamics between us, and part of it is between us and the rest of the world. For all of us, the hormones play a part though none of us can quite pinpoint what that part is.

Motherhood is a forever changing dynamic. Unconditional love is a constant, but the relationship shifts with each phase. At the moment, with teenagers, phases are coming thick and fast. Sometimes I think we may go through four or five in any one day. It's exciting, terrifying, rewarding and thankless, sometimes all at once. Are we setting each other off? In all likelihood, yes. Can we see it, stop it, head it off at the pass? No. Would we want to? Maybe – but it probably wouldn't be very helpful in the long run.

In recent years, I have sometimes felt like the manager of a football team, struggling in mid-season, or the colonel of a ragged battalion, a few years into a long campaign. I am doing my level best to deliver rousing team talks and wave the flag as I stride out. But I am increasingly just hoping rather than expecting that everyone is following me. I'm conscious that the flag is a bit tattered these days and reserves might be running low. A fog seems to have descended too so I really couldn't say with any certainty that I'm even facing in the right direction.

Interestingly, it is my part as would-be leader that is starting to feel redundant. The team members are – rightly and increasingly – full of energy and ideas about the best way forward. They don't always agree with me – or with each other. The playing field may well have changed. It is no longer up to me to decide the strategy.

Whilst I always knew that I wanted children, there is clearly no guarantee for any of us that we will be able to have them. For a while it looked as if I might not, but in the end I was lucky. Not all of the women I spoke to were, and in many ways the impact of that for some has increased as they have got older. Others chose not to have children. Others have lost children.

Whether we do or don't have children ourselves, by choice or not, our lives as women are shaped by the part that motherhood does, or does not, play. It is a role that is very difficult to ignore or be indifferent to over a whole lifetime for any woman. The intensity of emotions surrounding it, both positive and negative, can be overwhelming at times too.

I was very ready to listen to the experiences of women further along this path. Any insights were welcome.

The umbilical yank

Who could love my children as much as I do, with all their funny ways?
—Christine

The very gift of life is being snatched away from my daughter. I would give my life if I could. But I can't.
—Simran

My experience is that the umbilical cord is never cut. Occasionally you feel a tug, a yank. The umbilical yank.
—Liberty

If we are out walking in the spring, we sometimes come across a field of sheep with new lambs. They draw my attention. As I watch them, I feel a strong identification with the ewes. Some have momentarily lost sight of their lambs and are anxiously calling for them. Some are impatiently shifting their weight as the lambs jostle for prime feeding position. Some seem a bit shell shocked.

What I feel is a peculiar and fleeting bond with motherhood in another mammal. I recognise some of the purely biological instincts. My feelings are beyond reason in the same way that our reaction to pain or illness is. I understand why mother animals are often the most dangerous ones, the ones to give a wide berth to if encountered in the wild. I could be that animal if I needed to be.

I don't think I'm being too sentimental. After all, I still eat lamb. It's just that, in my experience, giving birth has stripped me back to my most basic biological self in some respects. Nature red in tooth and claw, and all that.

Sometimes this almost frightens me. It represents a one-way street of emotions, a life-long roller-coaster of love. I have stepped on and can never get off. Whatever happens, I will always feel that connection, the 'umbilical yank'. It's raw. It's powerful. It's uncontrollable. It's incredibly fortunate. It's a big responsibility. It's life.

An inexact science

Whenever we were unhappy with them, I used to say 'Parenthood isn't an exact science. I've never done this before. I don't know what other parents do, but I'm telling you now, I'm not happy.'
—Val

I was quite a disciplinarian. I'd be interested to know what they think now. I've never actually asked them, 'What are your recollections of how I did? Where did I fail?'
—Kitty

I think all parents do the best they can for their children. Though their children think they do everything wrong.
—Cecelia

In the first decade of motherhood, whilst I can't say I found it easy, I did feel an underlying confidence that I was on more or less the right lines. It seemed relatively straightforward to prioritise some basics such as sleep, vegetables and playing outside. Their grounded primary school head teacher used to say that there were three things we could do as parents to support them effectively: teach them to swim, give them some pocket money to manage for themselves and read with them. Great guidelines I thought. Now, I feel I can only hope that those years have laid a foundation that will prove to be a solid one.

Teenage-hood has brought exhilaration and despair, crippling anxiety at times, uncontrolled rage, highly articulated reasoning, unadulterated joy, over-analysing, not analysing enough, denial – for me as a parent as well as for them in the midst of this adolescent storm. It's brought an unexpected second viewing of my own teenage years, from a not entirely detached perspective, it turns out. I haven't done it, but I'm sure I could unearth some of my own teenage diaries and find almost word for word some of what my daughters tell me. And no doubt that goes back through generations before me too.

In the early years being a mother is a very physical role. It entails a close up on bodily functions that most of us have not had the dubious pleasure of before. There's a lot of literally heavy lifting. It's a full on sensory experience, caught up in the scents of babies, the feel of a small hand in yours, the sight of a warm sleeping body and a direct route to your sympathetic nervous system when they laugh or cry.

For me, it has become more complex, and more interesting, as they (and I) get older. Slightly to my surprise, I find I love having teenagers, even though it comes with a fair old measure of anxiety and irritation. The energy, enthusiasm, wit and challenge they bring make me laugh and sigh (sometimes at the same time). It's a very vivid stage of life, teeming with change at a sometimes eye-watering rate. I wouldn't miss it for the world, but being a good mother to a five year old requires different skills from being a good mother to a fifteen year old and, I imagine, from doing the same for a twenty five or fifty five year old child.

At the moment I find I'm hands off, hands on, uncertain when to be which and never being able to predict which might be needed. As soon as I resolve a more back seat role, something seems to happen that requires me to step forward. Once I get more involved, I can often sense a frustration both from me and them that it would probably be better if I would just get out of the way.

The fact is that there are no absolutes when it comes to this parenting lark. I found it reassuring to hear that in the conversations. Being a parent can challenge every opinion you have ever held and every certainty you thought you had nailed. Actually that feels to me like a healthy process. It keeps us all on our toes.

Like the women I listened to, I've done my best, and will continue to do so. What more is possible?

Independence and identity

Letting go is hard. I wonder what he's going to do next, but it's up to him now. You've got to trust them.
—Lesley

It's crucial to have your own identity as well as being a mother, and a wife. No matter what you do. You have to retain something of yourself.
—Val

Identity and independence work two ways. It is about both parent and child. Again, this is something that is relatively new for many women. Go back a century and I doubt women thought about this very much. Life took its course both for parents and offspring. Women didn't have a great deal of choice in the matter.

For my generation, technology has changed motherhood in relation to independence, our own or theirs. Every year the landscape changes a little more. It is different again even for parents of children a decade younger than mine.

We *can* be in close touch with our children as much as we or they like, wherever our children are and however old they are. I think this can add to existing pressures and can result in very real dilemmas about both a mother's own identity and the independence of their children.

This is recent. Even for me, when I went to university, I could only contact my parents by writing a letter or by queuing up to use a pay phone for a brief conversation. This was largely the same for anyone leaving home until a decade or so ago. Now, however, we can be in contact many times a day. It may be a mobile call or text, any number of other messaging apps, or indirect snippets of information gleaned via social media where it is easy to jump to conclusions that may not be accurate. What does it mean for me as a mother?

It's lovely. And potentially can be very limiting. Easier communication can enhance relationships with adult children no end. I also think it can be inhibiting, hindering the opportunities for young people to find a way of dealing with uncomfortable or difficult situations, or for ourselves to let them go.

I've watched parents – especially mothers – of young adult children diving into situations that I assumed twenty year olds did for themselves. It might be mothers advising about arguments with flat mates, acting as alarm clocks by ringing children to wake them up, reminding children of deadlines or completing forms for them. Those I have witnessed doing this have had demanding full time jobs, but before the day has started they have already dealt with one or two apparent crises in their children's lives. My husband, working for a global engineering firm, has seen an increase in mothers contacting him for work placement opportunities, on behalf of their son or daughter.

If parents swoop in to the rescue, crusader cape on, it doesn't let adult resilience develop. However, on the other side of the coin is the pull to protect at all costs. I understand the instinct very well. In addition, it is significant in busy lives that it is very often quicker and easier to sort out these issues ourselves, as soon as we hear about them. The difference for our generation is that we hear about them. Our parents usually didn't.

A few months ago, I was settling down to my day's work when I received a panicked and apologetic text from my daughter saying she'd dropped her bus pass on the way to the bus stop. I knew the route she'd walked (or actually run, being late) earlier that morning. I interrupted what I was doing, went out and found it. I felt relieved (it cost a bomb and getting a replacement is a hassle) and also irritated with the interruption.

But could I have carried on with my work, from my home office, knowing that a couple of hundred pounds worth of bus pass was probably lying a short distance away? I knew that it was an accident and that my daughter was upset about it. If I'd been somewhere else, the dilemma would not have arisen. But she knew I was working from home. It was easy (and sensible) for her to let me know. I'm glad she did. Once I knew, I felt it was worth nipping out to look. I'm not a mean person, and I love my daughter. We need to help each other. But is this the thin end of the wedge?

My generation of parents is possibly the first one to have to choose, consciously, to step back to allow independence to develop. It strikes me that this is a pretty tough place to be, probably for us and our children. My natural instincts are to help my children. I recognise that life isn't always easy for them. But I don't recall it being easy for me, or anyone else I know, at that age. Why do we think it should be?

This is a time when I need to allow, or even create, the space for them to face tough times and learn from them. They need to learn that they can recover from setbacks, deal with disappointment, and keep going even when that is the last thing that they want or feel able to do. But does that mean deliberately refusing to help in lost bus pass situations? It seems so harsh.

At the same time, there is me to think about. What about my identity and my work? My energy levels and concentration? The conversations all led to the same thing from women who had older children than I have; that it is important to hang on to your own identity and not to allow yourself to be overwhelmed by your children's lives. Sometimes, I have to say, it feels as if it is only hanging on by a thread.

The very act of writing is closely connected with this sense of identity for me. Writing a book is both a luxurious indulgence and an utter necessity to me. It's a way of carving out a creative and reflective space that is mine. I also feel like that about my work as a psychologist. I don't think it matters one jot what the activity is, and whether there's paid work involved or not. What seems to matter is maintaining something that is not purely about our children. It's important for us *and* them.

Qué será será

You may do the right thing or the wrong thing but in the end it will work out how it works out. It's quite hard to take that view.
—Lesley

It was a huge milestone when my children got married. I no longer felt totally responsible and stopped worrying about them all the time. I brought my children up in the age of helicopter parenting and we didn't stop hovering at eighteen.
—Nicole

I am beginning to realise that parts of my habitual motherly role are required less often as time goes on. I like to think that I will never be totally irrelevant of course but I am realising that not all decisions need to involve me and it's better for all of us if they don't. Trying to micro-manage children in their mid to late teens seems like a quest doomed to failure. Micro-management isn't my strong suit in any context anyway.

It is starting to occur to me that perhaps it's fine to sit down with a cup of tea from time to time and trust that all will be well. Or rather, whatever will be, will be.

I want to trust that all will turn out ok. In many ways there is nothing else to be done. And I also acknowledge that we can never say 'things turned out ok'. There's always some risk that something could go wrong. That's life. So as a mother, waiting until the point where 'everything turned out ok' before turning your attention to your own interests and life is likely to result in some missed opportunities.

The conversations showed me that it is possible to be yourself as well as never losing concern or interest in your children. It seems to require some wrenches along the way and some decisions about how to redefine the boundaries between ourselves and our children at different stages in life. This can be quite a challenge for both parents and children.

As a small example, I've started wondering how helpful the habit is of letting each other know we've arrived safely if we go on a longer journey. This is something my parents and I have always done. But if my children are away and they forget to text me, all I do is start to worry. The worrying doesn't change anything. It can't influence whether they actually got there safely or not.

I'm experimenting with not asking them to do that. I've found it means I don't think about their journeys as much. I still hear from them but not necessarily as soon as I think they should have arrived, and the messages I do get are friendlier and less dutiful. It means I'm less likely to try to calculate how long the journey should be, and second guess how it's gone. If something goes wrong, I'll hear about it when I hear about it. That's as it's always been, whether I expect them to call or not.

This seems symbolic of the bigger issues too. It seems very easy to set yourself up to worry fruitlessly by checking up on them for signs of happiness or health, or grilling them for information. The questions we habitually ask can be a real sign of our own anxieties rather than theirs. It's probably worth listening to ourselves.

It's not easy.

All or nothing

I don't want to get to eighty and think, I should have had children. I had a year of therapy because I really needed to explore this last chance to have a baby. I decided no. It just wasn't me.
—Anne

I would have loved having children. It's an empty blank space. I have found it more difficult as I've seen other people's children growing up and my chances got less. It feels like a big hole.
—Jane

He wanted children loads more than I did. It was a revelation to me how wonderful it was to have them and what a privilege and a joy. I was lucky because I needn't have had them and I wouldn't have known.
—Val

There seem to me to be few things in a woman's life that are quite as 'all or nothing' as having children. Whether you do or you don't, it can be defining. That choice isn't always under our control.

It took two years for me to conceive the first time, and at the time many of my friends were having babies. It was a difficult time in my life. How much more difficult it is for women who really want children and it doesn't happen at all, I can only imagine. It can be on-going heartache and can be just as difficult in later life, as they watch their friends become grandmothers. It can be equally hard for men too I think.

It's more of a taboo so we rarely hear about it, but I suspect there are also some women who *are* mothers and grandmothers who secretly wish they weren't.

However it turns out, having (or not having) children is life-changing and there are no half measures. No trial periods, no testing the alternatives. None of us can know what the road not travelled would have been like.

But, as the saying goes, it takes a village to raise a child.

Jane, who mourns the lack of her own children, has been instrumental in improving and saving thousands of children's lives by her work in children's health. She is a devoted aunt and great-aunt, which is an enormously important role for so many of us, both in childhood and as adults.

As a parent, I cannot begin to describe how important the other adults in my children's lives are – teachers, healthcare professionals, volunteers who run clubs, nursery staff, child-minders, neighbours, the extended family, and my friends. People behind the scenes, writing fiction for children or designing pushchairs. People who support me when I'm at a loss. People who listen to my children when they're not getting through to me.

We're all connected. We all benefit from children growing up to be functional adults. We can, and arguably should, all contribute to that process, parents or not. Handing over to the next generation, whether they are related to us or not, is both a skill and a blessing. It's a collective effort. Motherhood is only one part of that.

WHAT MATTERS

- Maintaining our own identity
- Doing our best
- Negotiating boundaries
- The support of 'the village'

WHAT DOESN'T

- Being in control all of the time
- Becoming more redundant – this is a sign of success
- Knowing what you're doing all the time
- The finish line – there isn't one

CHAPTER 6

WHO CARES?

Worry and the unknown – sadness – making hay while the sun shines – the shoebox – resilience – blessings – what matters – what doesn't

....

Being a carer.

How do you react to that phrase? Head in the sand? Hope your siblings will do it? Throw money at it? Cross that bridge when you get to it? Are you prepared to put your life on hold if you have to? Or perhaps you would welcome the chance to care for someone who once cared for you?

In the past, this has been a less visible issue than it is today. Families were often larger and more local. Caring for the sick and elderly was usually just one of the many things that women, and their communities, quietly got on with.

As we have seen, women's expectations are different now. I certainly have plenty of things that I want to do which don't involve being a full-time carer. I imagine most people feel the same. It's not something we usually choose to do in the way that we might make a decision to stop working and devote ourselves to parenting.

Unless we are somehow unconnected, lose our parents at a very young age, or deliberately distance ourselves – geographically or emotionally or both – most of us will probably need to become carers in some way, at some time. It's impossible to predict what form that will take, when it will be and how long it will go on for. It could involve caring for partners, friends, siblings or anyone else who falls ill, not necessarily just older relatives.

I watch my seventy-something parents take an increasingly complex cocktail of prescription drugs with their cornflakes when they visit. Both of them have had, and continue to have, serious as well as more minor health problems. They are both very active and independent despite all of that, and long may it continue, but I have twice been in a position to call an ambulance for my father, and my mother has Parkinson's disease. I know that the show goes on with a lot of support from our stretched but amazing health service. We are all grateful and impressed by the medical care they have received, over many years.

None of us know what lies further down the line. I alternate between refusing to torture myself with imagining multiple possible scenarios and, well, imagining multiple possible scenarios. I was keen to hear what the conversations would reveal.

Worry and the unknown

There's a background worry that always goes on. I pray fiercely that no disasters happen. There's always something. What you shouldn't expect is an expanse of time when there is nothing to worry about.
—Nicole

The worry, the anguish, the number of times I've driven back on the motorway in tears from visiting my mother has been awful.
—Jane

Worry is an odd process. It can get a grip so that it feels almost impossible to think about anything else. Some of us are very skilled at it and I know that I come from a background that is very adept at worrying. I've had good training.

However, most family events are never quite as you expect them to be. In fact that's true of most events in general. Listening to the conversations highlights to me what a waste of energy it is to try to second-guess what could happen. Gradually, needs may become more intense and more wide-ranging. There may be sudden changes. The whole range of emotions is likely to be involved. Logistically, already challenged juggling skills may need to become even more honed.

Or maybe none of the above. Or some of the above. Or something else. Who knows?

However, simply telling yourself not to worry doesn't work. I frequently come across this issue in my work as a psychologist. The more we tell ourselves or each other to stop worrying, the more intense the worry can become. This is often most vivid if you find yourself awake at night worrying about something. It's easy to end up upset and annoyed with yourself for blowing all sorts of things into insurmountable proportions at 4am. The annoyance doesn't shrink the worries though. If anything it magnifies them. Calm and sleep don't just return by ordering them to.

Research, and my own experience, suggests that, in the long term, mindfulness practice[3] can be one of the most effective ways of managing anxiety. In a nutshell, this helps to keep your attention in the present rather than dwelling on the past or making up things about the future. You learn to observe emotions and problems a little more rather than instantly trying to solve or eliminate them by sheer force of will.

All of our thinking about the future is actually about making things up. Our imaginations can come up with dramatic possibilities, especially in answer to the question 'what if?'. It doesn't usually feel like that, of course. It *feels* as if we are wisely predicting what will happen and therefore preparing ourselves, as the responsible adults we are, to deal with whatever we can foresee.

It is a useful skill to guess at the consequences of our actions and to forecast likely events. It helps us to carry an umbrella when need be or make financial decisions. It makes us think about how our actions now might influence our lives in years to come, and probably helps us not to smoke or drink too much.

But it can easily go too far. Our fertile imaginations get fuelled by strong emotions like fear and can go romping off in ever more vicious circles. Our guesses about the future seem like immutable facts and heighten the fear, turning it into dread. The fear keeps the imagination working overtime. Our impressive human mental agility takes a grain or two of truth and turns it into highly plausible illusion. Apply all this to what might happen to our loved ones and we can definitely keep ourselves awake at night. What if this, what if that? What will we do if....? How will I cope with....? What should I do about....?

The conversations showed me that it is nigh on impossible *not* to worry at all. I do, and will continue to, worry about my parents and my children. It's part of the package. There's something calming about accepting that rather than engaging in futile attempts to stop my worrier self in its tracks. It can be counter-intuitive.

But I also realised that the experience of caring that the women actually had, as events unfolded, wasn't predictable. Those who have been through it already have coped, whatever they might have thought about it beforehand. Those who haven't, or who are in the middle of it, don't know what the future holds any more than I do. And they are coping too.

It seems wiser to save energy for dealing with actual scenarios rather than using it up on imaginary ones. Directing energy towards building resilience – which we can do something about – is more positive. I'm not for a moment pretending this is effortless or straightforward. But this approach to the future is much calmer and likely to be much more productive, and this was reflected by many of the women as I listened to them.

Sadness

My mother's got dementia. It's really horrible. She's anxious the whole time.
—Anne

She just started fading. Her heart gave out. The older I get the more I miss my mum.
—Val

My daughter's situation is just awful to see.
—Simran

Along with, and sometimes aside from, the worry, is pure sadness about what can happen. A number of the women acknowledged and talked about these feelings, whether it was through caring or bereavement or both.

Within the conversations, this was never dwelt on at length. It was like a moment of distilled sadness, hanging like a fine mist of perfume that gradually dissipated to leave memories in its wake. I didn't try to probe further or to analyse.

This is life. If we're connected to people and love them, there will be an element of sadness. What I took from the conversations was an awareness that we shouldn't try to avoid sad or painful emotions. Some of the situations we encounter will be uncontrollable, some might be tragic. We can't alter this, though our presence and actions might help to alleviate the experience for others.

I can't say I'm looking forward to experiences like these, but I am less inclined to dread them now. The conversations have helped me to have a greater sense that, while difficult, they are part of the natural course of life and can't be avoided. They can't be pre-empted. They become part of who we are.

Making hay while the sun shines

We took my mum to New York. She was frail and stooped, and had her walker, so we went to the front of the queue for the open-top bus tour. My husband warned the kids we couldn't go upstairs, but whilst he was snapping the walker shut, she was like greased lightning on to the top deck.
—Kate

It can be easy to overshadow the present with worries about the future. And that can mean we are too tired or preoccupied to focus on what is possible right now.

The conversations brought this point up in many different ways, over a variety of topics. I reflected that the women who seemed to be most at peace with the way that events had turned out were those who had found ways of maximising opportunities for good times. They might be large or small events or moments. They provided experiences that serve as a buffer against sadder or more difficult times in the future.

In relation to caring, it seems to me that this can deliver benefits to both the carer and the person being cared for. It means there are positive memories in the bank.

On a practical note I think it is important to take photographs when possible. And not just take them, but also save, file, print and backup (ironically, all this is much more challenging in the digital age it seems). Having had two Golden Wedding celebrations in our family this year, we have seen first-hand how much pleasure it has brought to everyone involved to pore over pictures from the last fifty years. The photos taken at the parties are added to that stock. Nostalgia and reminiscence can be bonding as well as cheering.

I was aware that the women I was listening to all had very busy lives, in the same way that I do. Time hurtles past for all of us and it's shockingly easy to never get around to the things we would like to. It also never seems like a great idea to me to have a schedule so packed that there is no time to breathe (at least, that's not the way I function at my best). It means we need to take active steps to make opportunities to spend time with those people we would like to. Sometimes it feels more like a supreme effort, if we're honest.

I find I can't do this without robust diary management. My parents have a very busy social life (which is great) so meeting up with them for weekends involves careful diary comparisons. There's no sign of that abating just yet. Now that the children's schedules are filling up with activities that are their own – though still impact on my time at this stage of life – it's even more of a challenge.

But the effort is worth it. The conversations have confirmed that many times over.

The shoebox

Throughout being a single mum and caring for my mum, over about twenty years, I used to – metaphorically – put myself in a shoebox. I said to myself, you can't come out yet but you'll be fine.
—Liberty

I was very clear I couldn't look after my mother on my own. I was happy doing practical things and mental stimulation but I didn't want to do the intimate personal care.
—Kate

My three siblings and I all have a role in the care of my mother. I do all the health care stuff, the meetings with doctors, social services and so on. I go every week. It's been the most amazing emotional roller-coaster.
—Jane

Responsibility is an interesting concept, and one that gets called into question in any caring relationship. Arguments over responsibility can turn into major rifts in families, especially those under strain. And it can sometimes be a weight that people suddenly can't carry any more – at which point they may unexpectedly crumple.

When it comes to caring for others, I imagine it can be difficult to have clear conversations about who is responsible for which aspects. There can be a drive to take on responsibility for everything in an attempt to make things better. Likewise there might be all manner of expectations lurking in the family undergrowth ready to spring out shouting 'surprise!' when they are least welcome.

The conversations showed me that awareness of your own expectations and limits (both logistically and emotionally) is an important first step. There may be aspects that you definitely don't want anyone else to do, but see as firmly your role. And vice versa. From this starting point, conversations and negotiations can begin about who else does what, or what services might need to be paid for.

In addition, some sense of identity and self in the middle of it all seems essential to a sustainable caring role. Everyone has a different experience, but most of the conversations demonstrated a thoughtful series of decisions and negotiations with other family members and professional support that formed the bedrock of caring. The women themselves had made decisions about how often to visit or what their own involvement was. Part of this was about preserving a sense of identity that wasn't overwhelmed by caring.

Flexibility came across as a key attribute. The issue of flexibility is one that is especially tied to our personalities. Some of us like to plan and structure our lives whilst others like to be spontaneous. We all have to do a bit of both, like it or not, to navigate our way through life.

If you're the sort that likes to plan (and I have tendencies in that direction though they have mellowed a lot over the years – they've had to), it can be difficult to be faced with highly uncertain situations. I know I struggled with the complete unknowns about new babies and how long they might sleep, or when they would next need a feed. Friends of mine found that quite easy to adapt to, but were more challenged by the planning and structure involved in weaning or establishing bedtime routines.

We all muddled through one way or another. There is more than one way to care successfully, whether we're talking babies or the very elderly. I think that's the important element to remember.

Caring can be dauntingly hard work. I heard this several times during the conversations. My nervousness about that hasn't entirely subsided. But at the same time these were all women who had many interests, and numerous other things going on in their lives, alongside their caring roles. Somehow, the caring had not overwhelmed them, even though they may have felt or may still feel threatened by that on occasion. Simran has experienced a staggering twenty five years so far of extremely tough caring responsibilities, first for her husband and now her daughter. But she has been far from crushed by it from what I have seen. It must have come close at times.

I was calmed by the evidence in front of me that these women have not lost their marbles or their personalities. They still have active, interesting and enjoyable lives. They are realistic about what help is on offer and are prepared to seek and accept it when they can. They have a keen sense of their own capabilities. If they can do it, I'm reassured that I can too.

Resilience

Seven of my friends have elderly parents who need a lot of help.
They all work full-time. We go out and have supper together.
We call it our GGALs group (Girls Get a Life).
—Jane

When my dad was in hospital, I stayed there for about
three months. My husband came over to take me out at the
weekends. Just a walk round the park. I needed to breathe.
—Val

What many of the conversations reflected was that in
challenging times, anything that helps boost our resilience is
important. It may be the opportunity to sleep or exercise, or
paying attention to eating well. It may be listening to music or
audio books on multiple journeys. For some, it may be about
regular meditation, or perhaps religious practice. A supportive
social network helps enormously.

It's about being 'match-fit', to borrow a sporting term.
Rather than focusing on fearful visions of the future, it must
surely be more beneficial to apply ourselves to nurturing
resilience. We might need it at any time, for any reason. Dealing
with any of these caring scenarios when you are already lonely
or exhausted is going to feel overwhelming. There are too many
people of all ages in this situation already. They badly need a
helping hand.

But sometimes there is no immediate help on offer. If we can,
we need to help ourselves in that situation. It can feel selfish.
But – as with the instruction to fit our own oxygen mask before
helping others in an aeroplane emergency – if we don't look

after ourselves first, we'll be unable to look after others in the long term.

Mental and physical health is important for many reasons, but often we ignore it when we are busy or worried. I was reminded by the conversations how important it is to prioritise it in challenging times, and to allow our friends and family to help us.

I am making a mental note that if someone suggests a walk round the park or a meal together, the right answer is probably yes. Even – or perhaps especially – if circumstances are extreme. If no-one else is there to suggest, or insist, upon it, we need to try to do it anyway. It's not a selfish act. It is a vital ingredient of a caring role.

Blessings

I've been really lucky. I finished work at the time when my dad had his last big illness so I was able to be involved.
—Anne

My mum died this year. I was conscious of things like a need to take pictures of her hands. She raised seven children with them.
—Simran

Despite the hard work, the upset, the uncertainty and the worry, the women were clear about the value of being involved. Illness and end of life care are increasing pressures in our society, but at the same time they are a major and ever-present transition for all families, in all times.

Sickness and death are largely out of our control. They are frightening. It is not discussed properly or openly in the culture I live in. At a well-being panel discussion I attended recently, I remember being struck by a doctor raising the need for us, collectively, to consider what constitutes a 'good death'. It seemed such an important thing to say. Yes – on political and societal levels we have a serious need to face this question. And – yes, this also applies on a personal and family level.

I am sure I am not alone in my generation when I say I do not feel well equipped in this area. I do not know how to help any of my loved ones have a good death. Along with most people, I tend to shy away from the subject.

Over recent years, as a society, we seem to have improved the way we discuss birth so that women are better informed and prospective parents are better prepared for impact of a new baby. Television documentaries follow midwives and new parents. But I've been much less aware of a similar openness about long term illness and death, for the person themselves as well as the relatives, friends and professionals involved.

The conversations have helped challenge that taboo for me. Hearing about a range of experiences, in a very open and matter-of-fact way, has been helpful. I have also realised that I have a resource that I had not previously acknowledged. Older women. When the time comes for me to respond to the situations our family has to face, I am not alone. It's not always about seeking advice. It might be simply connecting with someone who has been there already and can understand what I'm feeling. Someone who can bring a longer term perspective.

I'm still apprehensive about what lies ahead. But I feel more positive and more philosophical about it now. The care process is not unremittingly negative. There are significant life-affirming aspects to it if we don't try to avoid or deny what's happening, and don't get too tired or overwhelmed.

WHAT MATTERS

- Keeping your metaphorical shoebox safe
- Making hay
- Clarity about roles and responsibilities
- Resilience
- Noticing and highlighting the positives

WHAT DOESN'T

- Predicting the future
- Worrying – it's inevitable to an extent, but let's not worry about worrying.
- A stiff upper lip
- Certainty – it's an illusion
- Too much emphasis on *what if?*

CHAPTER 7
WORK EXPERIENCE

Starting out – a woman in a man's world – living with the imposter – courage and drive – value and meaning – having it all – mid-life and beyond – what matters – what doesn't

....

When I was eight, I wrote to the Royal College of Nursing to ask them how to become a nurse. They wrote me a long letter and sent me a parcel of leaflets and information, and asked me to get in contact again when I was seventeen. It seemed a lifetime away at that stage. It still does, from another direction.

The pamphlets were well-thumbed in those pre-internet days. I also devoured Helen Dore Boylston's *Sue Barton* stories – a series which took our heroine through a romanticised nursing career. I was keen to get started.

Years passed. I decided that instead I wanted to be a dietician. Food has never been far from my mind. However, the necessary advanced level chemistry proved to be less than appealing, so I shifted focus again. When I finally reached the magical seventeen, I applied to study psychology at university.

Life didn't go in an obviously straight line for me. In the interests of earning a living, I went into accountancy after university. By now I had ventured a long way from my original ideas. I was a square peg in a round hole at that time, it has to be said. But I have never regretted it. It was challenging – long hours, copious exams of the most intimidating variety, and a perceived requirement to stride through the corporate world in a suit. It never felt quite like the real me. But it was unbeatable experience. The training was rigorous and I saw a huge range of organisations at first hand. I felt a massive sense of achievement when I finally became chartered. The unexpected bonus came in the form of lifelong friendships forged in those days.

With thirty looming, and realising it was the people rather than the numbers that I found most interesting, I went back to university to study occupational psychology. It's what I've been doing ever since. It can take a while to find a niche.

Perhaps because it seemed to take me so long, and also because I have chosen to spend the years since then bringing up children as well, I sometimes have a sense that my work has barely started. Hitting my stride can be a frustratingly elusive experience. There is always something else to do as well. I know I share that feeling with many other women.

Work can be a necessary evil or the most rewarding and meaningful experience. It can feel as if it has taken over the rest of our life or has given purpose to it. In general, work is good for our mental health. Not having enough to do, or feeling as if we have no purpose, can be a lonely and stressful place. Of course, it can be equally stressful to be overloaded.

The conversations revealed a fascinating patchwork of work-related experiences. The women have held a wide variety of jobs and voluntary roles and worked in many different organisational settings. For me, hindsight has been more useful than planning to make sense of my career path. I was really interested to find out what it was like for my women.

Starting out

I left school at fifteen and said I wanted to work in a shop. The man at the labour exchange said, there's a job in the calendar factory. That was it. My mother said, that'll do.
—Pat

I didn't pass many of my A levels – so at eighteen I went to London to get a job. I collected rents and did assessments for the housing department of Westminster City Council. It was a real eye-opener.
—Marie

I finished my art foundation course and worked as a bar maid in various places for about a year. I was desperately shy. It gave me the skills I needed for later when I had to step forward.
—Helen

When I looked back at all twenty conversations, I was struck by how modest the beginnings were for almost all of the women. Even the ones who ultimately had very successful professional careers either fell into their training almost as a default action as they knew they had to do *something*, or took quite a few years to find their way to the necessary education and training.

I found this heartening. It was unusual in my group of twenty for them to know what they wanted to do at seventeen and then follow that path with no changes in direction. Not only did it echo my experience, it has also helped me to worry less about my own teenagers. Most of the women could see significant benefits to the experience they gained at an early stage, whatever it was. Listening to them, I realised my own unplanned career route is not as wayward as it may have felt whilst I was blindly going through it.

I have long had a sense, from working with a range of different clients as a psychologist, that nothing is wasted in terms of experience. Even when we are employed in jobs that seem mundane or unrelated to subsequent careers or direction, there is nearly always something about them that becomes a valuable piece in the jigsaw. The conversations confirmed this over and over again.

The starting point may or may not bear much relation to the end point of a career. Jane went into nursing because she didn't feel able to follow her academic parents and siblings to university. She took time out after qualifying to do something completely different – an interesting interlude working with actor and politician, Glenda Jackson, as her assistant, as it happens (one of those happenstance opportunities). Persuaded to go back to nursing by the Matron who clearly saw her potential, she has ultimately become one of the most senior and influential nurses in the UK.

Linda started on the shop floor of a lingerie factory at fifteen and became a highly successful fund-raiser, educator and local business champion, all in her home town of Nottingham. Helen's work started behind the bar, and went through many changes in direction and location before becoming a director of a textile company. Marie went on from rent collector to become a Partner in a global accounting firm.

The starting point is not the biggest barrier to career progress. Personally, I suspect this still holds true today, despite the pressure that seems to be loaded on to our young people (and their parents). The biggest barriers seem to be our own beliefs and motivation.

I am not saying that anything is possible if you want it enough. That can be a damaging expectation, boosted by seemingly endless competitive reality television shows. It is a fragile illusion that can lead to hopeless despair in the face of real life. Hopeless despair is a much more difficult starting point than disappointing exam results or a menial job.

These women are real. Their experience shows us that enthusiasm, courage, responding to opportunities and sheer hard work can take us a long way from where we started if we want them to.

A woman in a man's world

It may not be a great achievement by other people's standards but I was the first woman to be Church Secretary.
—Margaret

I remember going to a meeting, where there were about 350 men in the room and me. The only other woman was serving the tea. I asked her to sit next to me!
—Linda

There are very set ideas about how women should be – that they should be decorative.
—Jeannie

Times are changing. Or are they?

It depends on our field or organisation, but in many arenas women are not equally respected or represented. The women I listened to were quietly ground-breaking in some instances.

Even in voluntary roles, I was struck by how those with most status were still – by and large – taken by men.

Some of the women had attended state funded girls' grammar schools, as did I. These women often reported a strange mix of expectations from their teachers, from that era. They were expected to go on to higher education but this would be constrained to traditional subjects. A limited range of careers were considered acceptable for women – teaching, or a healthcare profession such as physiotherapy. Some schools simply refused to support ambitions beyond this. Val, for example, did teacher training with art – her school refused to supply a reference for her to go to art school.

These attitudes had mellowed by the time I was at secondary school, although some teachers held convictions that I didn't share. My school reluctantly allowed me to mix arts and sciences at 'A' level for instance but only on condition I accepted their opinion that I was unlikely to have a career as a result. It was a disheartening prediction for a sixteen year old.

We all know that even today, there are areas where women are breaking new ground, being the first or amongst a tiny minority to undertake certain roles. They are often in the spotlight – for being women – whether they like it or not, and may be the subject of vociferous opinion, good and bad. I am reminded of the reaction to the first women to enter the Olympic boxing ring – in 2012.

It can put women in an uncomfortable and isolated place. I remember being the only woman in some audit teams during my accountancy years. Sometimes the client organisation's workforce was very male-dominated too, especially those operating in heavy industrial areas.

Whilst I don't remember any malicious discrimination, from either colleagues or clients, I do remember the more subtle elements. At the time, women were not allowed to wear trousers in the firm I worked for (I can barely believe that, looking back). We usually had numerous files and bags to carry. I nearly always found myself tottering across the car park in heels and skirt with armfuls of paperwork, behind my more junior male colleagues. They leapt out of the car and marched ahead in wholly functional clothes, oblivious. On several occasions, the client management waiting to greet us assumed that the people who reached the door first were the most senior. My opening greeting then had to be something to do with correcting that assumption. It never felt like an authoritative start.

I can also remember some awkward Friday lunchtime pub visits with colleagues and clients, as the only woman. If the conversation turned to football or – worse – women, they had often by then forgotten I was there. It didn't happen that often, but some of those mealtimes were a challenge. I didn't know how to deal with it. I usually just kept very quiet, concentrated on my chips, and waited for it to pass.

It felt reassuring in some ways to hear that I was not the only one, and that variations on this theme had been experienced by some of the women I listened to. I used to think I should try to be a different kind of person. Perhaps I should mug up on football and become one of the lads, or come across as a tough woman that my male colleagues were slightly scared of. But those alternatives just weren't me.

They still aren't. I am light years further on in being comfortable in my own skin compared with those days. What I have learned from the conversations is that being the lone woman in a group of men can often feel uncomfortable, and it's not just me that feels that way. This may well be the case for a lone man in a group of women too. It's just that in many workplaces this is a less likely scenario, especially in more senior settings.

Both men and women need to be aware of the subtle ways in which they might exclude people on the basis of their gender. And if we are in the minority, the conversations have shown me that it is important not to let it put us off.

Living with the imposter

When I opened the letter offering me a Dameship, I thought it was a joke. The shock of it was enormous. I still expect someone to tap me on the shoulder and say, 'Nurse, get back in the sluice, and start cleaning the bed pans.'
—Jane

I got the job. I was dumbstruck. I thought I hadn't got a hope in hell.
—Linda

I'm eternally grateful to my dad for saying, go for it. I was amazed I even got called for interview. It was gruelling. But then I realised I'd got the job. So I went to Iran. I was 23.
—Tanje

I sometimes have doubts about whether I'm a good psychologist or a good writer. The conversations have shown me that similar feelings are common for these women. It would be highly unlikely – and arguably, undesirable – that I could be working in either field without a few qualms now and then.

Some – many, actually – felt a sense of 'imposter syndrome', a fear that somehow they weren't as good as other people thought they were and that one day they would be 'found out'. I know from my work as a psychologist that this is not unusual. Scratch the surface of many a successful person and there lies a fear of being exposed as a fraud. The more ambitious and demanding the job, the more complex it is likely to be and the more opportunities for doubt will creep in. The stakes might not only feel higher, they might actually be higher. It can be stressful.

However, it can be reassuring to know that other successful people share these feelings. Perhaps, to some extent, they are essential for us to do a good job. Those who never doubt whether they are up to the task may be disastrous employees in some environments.

Within reason, a degree of stage fright (whatever our field) can be a good thing. It can sharpen our senses and get our adrenaline running just enough to help us step up – often higher than we thought we could. Confidence comes as a result of doing things rather the other way round. That's not how we usually regard it. We imagine that other people do things because they feel confident before they start. The conversations have confirmed that this is not the case at all.

Courage and drive

We all need courage to do our jobs well.
—Jane

I got a job managing children's homes. I was far too young, looking back. I was supposed to drive and I couldn't.

No one wanted a woman in the job. But I did have good management experience and experience of working with very difficult children.
—Kate

For me, my energies were very much about my career. That became everything for me. I was somehow balancing my children's needs, my husband's needs and my own needs because I was getting fulfilment from my career.
—Simran

It takes tenacity, as well as trial and error, to discover our aptitudes and decide how we want to use them. I think that I left school assuming that my abilities were relatively fixed by then. I guess I felt that I had been judged and assessed so much by then that there wasn't much more to say.

This assumption is very limiting. If that's it, well – that's it. As a psychologist, I have since learnt that mindset is more important than objectively measured abilities at a point in time. Stanford University psychologist, Carol Dweck (author of *Mindset – the new psychology of success*), is interesting and influential in this area. A growth mindset – where you believe that it is possible to learn and develop throughout life – leads to greater resilience than a fixed mindset when faced with setbacks. It means we are likely to put more effort into learning new skills and are ultimately more successful.

As I listened to my women, I realised that many of them exhibited exactly this. They went into situations they were not sure they could handle or were outside of their experience. They had a readiness to learn, and a belief that they *could* learn, painful though that might sometimes be. It takes courage and drive.

By taking this approach, they expanded their horizons in ways they had not expected. One opportunity – or person – led to another. It was exciting, interesting, and scary at times. And potentially very rewarding.

Value and meaning

If you give in to truly being yourself, your work is you, and being you will give you the work. I can't think of any other way to put it.
—Liberty

I was a home help. People were pleased to see me. Just doing a job for money is not good because you're going to spend so much of your life doing it.
—Pat

Work was always very important to me. Following my research job, I worked at a local college. I went down a grade because there wasn't the money, but I wanted the experience. I like my work.
—Christine

Value and meaning were frequently mentioned by the women who were positive about their work. It has given them purpose and identity which is separate from their roles as mother, grandmother, daughter or wife.

I know that not everyone wants, or needs, this in the same way. Some women are perfectly content with their other important roles. Some are content with them at some stages of their life and then want different things at other stages. I applaud this whole range of choices and preferences. The world would be a very much poorer place if we were all the same.

I have always wanted to maintain a career alongside my roles as mother, wife and daughter. Equally, I have been very committed to giving as much time and attention as I can to bringing the children up. There is always a tension between these two things, whatever we do. Now that my children are nearing adulthood, I was particularly interested in hearing from the women who had kept their career ticking over whilst raising children. What happens next, as the balance gradually shifts away from hands-on parenting?

Some of the women used this time as an opportunity to go in a new direction, and some used it to develop new areas of interest. I was encouraged by their enthusiasm and energy for getting stuck into whatever they did from my age upwards. I recognise that the people who find their niche are tremendously fortunate. Not all of my women felt that they had done so.

But if we want to find it, the message seems to be that it is rarely too late to try. Realistically, the number of options may diminish as the years pass, but probably not as much as we think they do. If we don't ask, or have a go, at the things that interest us, how do we know what the barriers are? And once we know what they are, we might be able to do something about overcoming them.

Of course, not everyone is on a quest to find their niche. Some are very content with a bearable job that pays the bills. In many ways I have felt envious of that on occasions, especially in some of my more tortuous years when I have undoubtedly made life more difficult for myself with some of my decisions.

We're all different. The thing I have come away with from the conversations is that time spent understanding what makes you tick – at any age – is time well spent. What adds value and meaning to our lives? It could be any number of things – relationships, voluntary or creative projects, paid employment – and it may be different things at different stages of our lives. I have learnt that we should expect it to take some courage, a sprinkling of good luck and quite a lot of experimentation to find out. It's not a comfortable process.

There seems to be no stopping the women who understand themselves in this way. Whatever form it takes, if they have found their niche, they are up and running with it, regardless of age. It was good to hear.

Having it all

I was determined not to give up the acting business when I had children. That's when I auditioned for BBC Radio and got into the schools section. I was marginalised but I never gave it up.
—Jeannie

I couldn't have my old job back because you weren't allowed to if you were married.
—Tanje

I haven't been terribly ambitious. I didn't work until the youngest children were six or seven. I went part time to work at the local college. It was nice work.
—Rose

I grew up at a time when there was a great deal of talk about women 'having it all'. I don't think it's possible, certainly not all at once. If we try, we generally risk burning out in the process. But from listening to the conversations, it seems apparent that many women can and do flex what they do and how they do it, and have different priorities at different times in their lives.

Women are often balancing work with other aspects of life, and in my case this is the result of *wanting* to do just that. This means I am not a single-minded career person. I am not a single-minded mother either. Like many women, I am not very single-minded about anything, longer term. Life is too interesting for that, to my mind.

I want to do a range of things. I want to see my friends and family, and I want to stay fit. I want time to read and write. I want to continue to develop as a psychologist. I want to sleep, and chill out in cafés. I like cooking and sometimes knitting. I want to do something locally on a voluntary basis (currently as a school governor). I love going to the cinema and theatre. I don't want to work all waking hours in one single endeavour, whether that is motherhood, work or anything else.

I have always felt quietly ambitious, not for conventional status but for helping people and making a difference. For applying psychology as best I can. These phrases sound a little tired and hackneyed even as I write them. But I'm not sure how else to put it.

Listening to my women, the fortunate ones are those who are either quite content with their lifestyle and choices, or those who have burning questions to answer or a creative urge that they have long waited to satisfy. Neither group is bored.

However, it's not purely down to good fortune. The women in these groups have been lucky to have some opportunities, but they have also worked hard to overcome circumstantial and psychological obstacles on the way. They have often learned to be good at counting blessings and recognising the ingredients of contentment for them. They are good at distinguishing between what is under their control and what isn't. They've taken risks. It usually hasn't been an effortless or smooth path to where they are now.

There have been years when these women have prioritised one role over another, not always by choice. Sometimes that has meant keeping their hand in with some roles rather than letting them go altogether. Sometimes it has meant leaving paid work for a while, or doing a job that is convenient, or that fulfilled some needs but not all.

From what I heard, it wasn't ever about having it all, all at once. Something always took a back seat whilst other things came forward. But over a lifetime, that seems to be a successful strategy. It puts a much less frantic spin on it than trying to keep all of the balls in the air, all at the same time.

There is room for a whole variety of working patterns, caring responsibilities, and voluntary or creative roles over the course of a lifetime. It unfolds over many years. Things change over time in ways we can't predict. Opportunities can crop up unexpectedly. The closest we can come to 'having it all' seems to be in taking the long view.

Mid-life and beyond

In my fifties, I retired from that job and started following the things that are great for me. It became the platform for the next ten years of really brilliant stuff.
—Marie

I decided I needed a new job when I was fifty. It was the most vulnerable time of my life. I thought, this is the time when I am going to find out if I – on my own – am of any value.
—Madeline

I still like to have an objective, something to aim for.
—Kitty

The conversations confirmed my hunch that the impact that women can make through work is far from over, and in fact may only just be beginning, as we reach our fifties. Several told me about interesting and exciting new directions since traditional retirement age, and certainly since turning fifty. Especially for those with a creative bent, the work is not age related – or if it is, it seems to be positively correlated with age.

Some ideas have been incubating for years if not decades for these women. It is sometimes only in later life that the space and opportunity arises to put them into action. To be put into words or pictures or deeds or gardens. The message is clear – it is rarely too late. The women I spoke to who are well into their eighties are still very actively involved in their communities and dearest held projects and interests. They have plans.

My feeling is that for many women, our life's work is truly life-long. Women can and do come into their own at any age. Despite our society's tendency to highlight youth, older women are doing some amazing things, sometimes from a very late start or change in direction.

We are perhaps less constrained than the men in our lives by ideas of what retirement is, or maybe we are ready to pick up the pace or change direction after we've experienced the limitations that come with caring for children or other people.

Post-menopausal women are certainly not ready to throw in the towel from what I've heard. Very far from it – and I am relieved and inspired to hear it.

....

WHAT MATTERS

- Mindset and motivation
- Taking risks
- Spotting and responding to opportunities
- Understanding what makes you tick
- Flexibility

WHAT DOESN'T

- Straight line progress
- The starting point
- Having it all, *at the same time*
- Hard and fast plans
- Being able to control everything

CHAPTER 8

THE ROOT OF ALL EVIL?

The long shadow – earning – spending – managing – independence – pensions - how much is enough? – what matters – what doesn't

....

My first experience of paid work was a fortnight spent on an archaeological dig when I was fifteen. Growing up near Colchester, Britain's oldest recorded town, it was impossible to be unaware of archaeology. Nothing was built without investigating what was underneath the ground. And when a dig sprang up amongst the crops in the fields near my house, it didn't seem that strange.

Urged by my parents, I eventually approached and asked if I could join in. They said yes. I put on my wellies and learned the all-weather arts of practical archaeology – removing tons of top soil, making tea in makeshift sheds for armies of people, and emptying portable toilets. It wasn't glamorous, but it was great fun. It also involved patiently and delicately scraping away at the earth in the hope that the pattern that the experienced archaeologists could see would eventually reveal itself to me too. I sometimes caught a glimpse.

It was an eye opening experience on many levels. My inner hippie revelled in it. I was endlessly fascinated by the variety of nomadic eccentrics, straight scientists and earnest historians who were attracted to this kind of work. My imagination was fired up by the idea of the communities who had lived in that spot of unremarkable English farmland all those centuries ago. It was easy to imagine ghosts when the light was in a certain direction.

But the most surprising element for me happened on the Friday afternoon when everyone queued up to get paid. On the first Friday, I stayed where I was, trowel in hand and dreamily scratching away. And then someone came to tell me to collect my wages too. I was shocked. I went to the shed assuming I'd get a token amount and was given an envelope with £25 in cash in it – which was the same as everyone else. I couldn't believe it. It was more money than I'd ever had at once and it was all mine. It happened again the following week.

Would I have approached the dig had I expected to be paid? Probably not. I had no experience, no idea what they were looking for or whether they had vacancies, no confidence that I could deliver what they needed or wanted, and, certainly at that age, no sense that I was entitled to ask.

When I look back at myself from today's vantage point though, I realise that of course I had plenty to offer and did in fact earn that money as much as anyone else did. I hefted barrow loads of soil around with the best of them. I washed pottery and carefully labelled it with a fine ink pen (a deeply satisfying job). I took my turn with the tea and the toilets. I kept going through wind, rain and blistering sunshine for the same number of hours that everyone else did. I learned what a mattock was and how to wield it. I learned how to trowel. I was interested in (though a bit baffled by) what they told me we were finding.

The same hesitancy about money has accompanied me all my life. Money is a vexed issue for me. Earning it, or spending it. But financial issues are rarely simply about coins, notes and numbers. Particularly in the work arena, what we earn, expect to earn, demand or ask to earn is often about the value we put on ourselves. The same can apply when it comes to spending it, especially on ourselves.

I don't think that any of the women I interviewed would consider themselves to be poor in their older years. All are warm enough and well-fed. Some are, I think, relatively wealthy.

It's not always been that way for most of them though, and many describe very difficult financial circumstances in their childhood or younger years. Their parents' experience was often tied up with the Depression and wartime. My own parents were children during the Second World War. It has had a major impact on their approach to money and resources in general.

They still keenly remember rationing, and both were in families running on uncertain incomes from small businesses. My father's father died during the war and my grandmother was left with a tiny income from her part time work as a school dinner lady, and some help from National Assistance, to bring up two children (no widow's war pension – a story of injustice for another time). It's inevitable that there is a legacy of all this, one way or another.

Our feelings about money are a result of the culture we are born into and our family's approach to money. Our own patterns may duplicate what we've seen or react against it. As women, we learn a lot from how our mothers, grandmothers and other significant women have dealt with money in the context of long term relationships or managing on their own. How we define how much money is enough is an interesting topic, as is how we form our perceptions of what we consider to be well-off or hard-up.

I have been amused, impressed, alarmed and amazed by some of the tales of financial history that have come up in the conversations. I have had a peek into a world that is not often discussed.

The long shadow

When he was unemployed, my grandad refused to accept food vouchers. They had a 7 year old child, a one year old baby, a Spanish refugee – and no money. Grandma got the voucher, against his wishes, and he went bananas. She hit him over the head with the remainder of the meat she had been given!
—Linda

I remember Mum carrying two suitcases of our old clothes into town to sell in the second hand shop. They said the clothes weren't good enough, and she had to carry them all the way back. She was so upset. It didn't last long but there have been hard times. It's the only time I felt threatened by the lack of money.
—Margaret

My mum had to leave school at eleven to earn money for the family because her father couldn't get work in the Depression. She had a scholarship for the grammar school but never went.
—Helen

I was brought up in a self-employed household, as were both my parents. This meant we all had an acute awareness of the link between work and money, as nothing was earned in down times. No paid holiday or sick leave. No redundancy opportunities. Not much in the way of pension provision. I have chosen the same path, as I am also self-employed. For a period of time I was also the breadwinner in a single parent household.

I have experienced the feast and famine that is so typical of small businesses, just about all my life. Some years have been very good, others less so. I've never really learnt to trust money. If I'm earning it now, I tend to assume there's a lean period coming up. If I'm not earning much, I expect this state of affairs to continue indefinitely.

This has led to a collection of varied beliefs about money, and, now, I can see more clearly where the roots of this might be. My parents felt that spending on clothes, appearance, exotic travel and frequent meals out were extravagancies. In general, we didn't do them.

My childhood holiday diaries are littered with the calm statement that 'We went to such-and-such but didn't go in'. I can remember travelling slowly up long driveways and approaches to various tourist attractions, only for the car to be turned around when we got close enough to see what the entrance fee was. I don't remember minding that much. And as a parent, I truly do understand, and I have done versions of the same thing. Some of these things do feel like daylight robbery.

I *do*, however, remember minding when we didn't visit the café if we were on an outing. Some of my favourite memories stem from when this restriction was lifted and we spent a summer evening in a pretty pub garden, or had coffee or ice-cream in a seaside café (still right near the top of my list of treats). Or we'd maybe buy a bag of chips, wrapped in newspaper, on the way home. It all seemed so much more exciting than brewing up tea in a windy layby on a portable gas ring (it's a long time since I've seen someone doing that).

I have fond memories, as a very young child, of weekly shopping trips with my mother, which often involved a rest in a 'drinks shop' (I think it was usually a branch of the legendary tea shop chain, Lyons). Fair play to my mother when I think back. The grocery shop involved buses and walking, all done with a gigantic pram laden with children and potatoes. Frankly, it's a surprise that we didn't go into a 'drinks shop' which offered something a little stronger than tea.

There were another couple of notable episodes of unforeseen spending in my childhood. Once, my father came home from the accountant, having confirmed that he had had a good year, with a gift to himself of a second-hand banjo (he likes and appreciates music but isn't a musician himself). Another time, my brother and I were told we had to be at home for a 'wood delivery' which turned out to be a second-hand piano. Both incidents left me feeling excited and surprised by this sudden and completely unexpected loosening of the purse strings. The world suddenly seemed full of possibilities. Mostly of a musical nature it would seem.

Further back in my ancestry, I come from non-conformist protestant - at one time, Scottish Presbyterian – stock. This has left us all with a legacy that money is to be treated with caution and suspicion, and with respect and contempt in equal measure. Images of camels and eyes of needles, and overturned tables in temples, are never too far away. I am expected to deal with money sensibly and frugally. On the whole, I have always done exactly that.

The conversations have shown me the close link between our backgrounds and our habitual attitudes to money. It's fascinating, and makes it impossible to have a neutral or indifferent relationship with money.

Earning

If I do it voluntarily and I'm not paid, I'll have a go at anything. I pulled an ailing magazine out of huge debt on a voluntary basis. But if I'd seen an ad for a job doing the same thing for money, I would never have tackled it.
—Tanje

The job came up and I got it. Actually, I'm not very confident and I spent those years feeling unworthy. The motivation? Money.
—Anne

I used to work at the cattle market on a Saturday, making tea and sandwiches for the farmers. I earned about five shillings and I had to give my mother half of it. It made me think about money rather than keeping it all to myself.
—Pat

On the earning side, I know that my father was never keen to market his skills actively. He worked as a graphic designer, with clients including our local theatre, some high-end restaurants and a large wine merchant. All of his clients had come through word of mouth. From an early age, even though I couldn't have described it in these terms, I got the impression that he didn't really want to join in the capitalist consumerist setup of which we were unavoidably a part. I always rather admired that slightly rebellious streak, whilst feeling frustrated by it at times. As a talented artist too, he was, and still is, reluctant to put his work up for sale, or find a commercial outlet for his undoubted creative abilities. The business thrived with my mother at the book-keeping helm, but it seemed to me as if he was almost making a living in spite of himself. It was akin to trying to drive with the brakes on, and I think we all felt that in our different ways.

And guess what? In many ways, I am *exactly the same*.

I allow myself some impulse buys when I feel that things are going well (even so, I haven't got a banjo yet). I never trust that money will continue to come in. I'm wobbly about selling.

And I don't think I actually share this with my father but I know I have had an unhelpful belief , never too far away, that I don't deserve to earn well. The conversations are helping me to – at long last - challenge that belief. I often prefer to be paid as an unexpected bonus rather than as a right (the dig all over again). Have I developed this idea partly because I am a woman? Perhaps my earnings are 'ill-gotten gains'. It was an oft-used joke phrase in our household as I was growing up. Doesn't seem quite so funny, as I reflect on it from here.

It is tricky to measure many of our achievements objectively. For me, valuing psychology and writing in financial terms is difficult. In publishing alone, some books, generally considered to be poorly written, may sell in their millions, while some books with acclaimed critical recognition just don't sell at all. Some become popular years or even decades after they were written. Cash and value are not always clearly linked. Who decides what is good and what isn't, or what the price tag should be? It leaves me feeling confused and tentative. I know I'm not the only psychologist or author to feel this. Or the only woman.

I know exactly what Tanje means about tackling challenging jobs on a voluntary basis. It feels safer somehow. I also know what Anne means about sticking with a difficult job for the money. I've done both of those things.

My family's approach to earning money is clearly not wholly dysfunctional. We have always been solvent, had a solid roof over our heads and dinner on the table. In world-wide and historical terms, we are in an enormously fortunate and shockingly tiny minority that hasn't had to worry about going hungry or simply surviving.

But the conversations have led me to reflect that valuing our own time and effort, and wanting to be paid fairly for our contributions, in whatever field, is important - particularly if older women are to make the impact that they could.

Our attitudes to earning money are about so much more than cash and they can limit us from contributing to our world in the way that we can, and arguably, should. Looking around me, if there was ever a time when older women, such as those I have spoken to, are needed to make a difference in the world, it must be now. They can't all do it on a purely voluntary basis, willing though most of these women are to give their time and expertise for free.

And beyond the money we might *need*, there is the self-respect and value from others that comes from earning a reasonable sum for a good job. This is the aspect that I struggle with most and, judging by the conversations, I'm not alone. I don't like the fact that people's contribution is often more highly valued because they are paid well, and they exhibit outward signs of that in the form of good clothes and belongings. I wrestle hard with the concept. My inner hippie – who has never gone too far away – doesn't see why this should be the case at all.

But in practice, I have experienced an increased level of interest from all sorts of people (including those I suspect of having their own inner hippie) when they realise that I'm being paid well for some work. Without that, I think there is an assumption that I am just indulging a hobby. With money in the equation, people seem to sit up. Maybe this makes them think I'm doing something the world wants. It must matter because people are paying for it. I sometimes find myself responding like that too, to friends or acquaintances. I don't like it but there it is.

I've always wished that I could somehow transcend the problematic question of earning money. I fondly imagine it would be nice just to do the work I feel is important, and that I am suited to, without measuring its worth in financial terms. Maybe in some other time and place this is possible, but it isn't in the world that I, and my women, inhabit.

I dream, maybe completely erroneously, that a huge windfall such as a lottery win would bring financial liberation (I have never bought a lottery ticket, however, so this fantasy can continue to exist unchallenged). The idea of sudden unexpected wealth has never been equated with giving up work in my mind, but with enabling bigger and better work. Perhaps I should be a philanthropist when I grow up, or when my fantasies miraculously spring into life. Whichever happens first.

The conversations have shown me that, in relation to money, the opposite of cautious and hesitant is not necessarily boastful and selfish, which I think has been my fear. Instead, it can be modest, useful and generous. When I think of the women I talked with, I am delighted by the many examples where they have had the courage to put themselves forward for important work, and have valued themselves enough to be well-paid for what they've done.

It has brought the world into contact with their art, their expertise, and their good ideas. Being paid for it has made their contribution sustainable and enabled them to do more, and have more influence, than they would probably have been able to do on a voluntary basis. If they had hung back, assuming their ideas and skills were of little financial value, the world would be a poorer place. If they (or I) hang back it will mean that people who might greatly benefit from our products or services will never have heard of us. Is it modesty, fear, or possibly misplaced rebelliousness, that keeps me from setting out my stall?

The conversations have been a very useful step in helping me to examine my own conflicted thinking. I think it's an area where I will always feel ambivalent to a degree. But knowing that I'm not alone, and that there are women modelling a much more constructive approach, is empowering.

Spending

Spending doesn't make you happy but investing does.
—Helen

I was just raised to not consider that I should spend money on myself. Even when I earned I didn't buy myself things.
—Linda

When I started work, I remember eating chocolate on the train on the way home. I thought, where's all my money gone? It's all gone on Mars bars!
—Cecelia

By now, you won't be surprised to hear that I have had problems on the spending side of the equation as well as the earning side. I allow myself to spend on some items and not others. The 'allowed' list includes good food and groceries, cultural and educational experiences and books (and yes – drinks shops). 'Not allowed' often includes clothes, make-up, expensive meals out and travel. I don't think I need to spell out where this comes from. It works, after a fashion, but it's not always very rational.

But again, what a relief to hear some of these same mixed feelings from the women in the conversations. It is a complicated area for many of us. I do not want to be penny pinching, mean, scared, inward-looking, sorry for myself, and driven by austerity. I am learning that this mindset just shuts everything down. It's one thing recognising it though, and another thing doing something about it.

I've wondered, since the conversations, whether the income and the expenditure side go hand in hand psychologically. Perhaps it is impossible to have a highly cautious, defensive attitude to earning, woven through with an underlying despair about future income, and a happy-go-lucky view about spending. Vice versa, perhaps it is not possible to keep a lock down stance on spending and simultaneously be connecting and reaching out in terms of building my business and earnings.

I have never thought about this in quite this way until now. But how do I go about changing such long-term views, which – to be fair – have served me well enough? I have never been in debt beyond the mortgage, and have never been hungry. That counts for quite a lot.

I am also very well aware of the problems brought about by compulsive spending for the sake of it, both psychologically and financially. I don't want to grow my business into something that I am managing rather than doing. Whilst I am in no way an ascetic, I am not very materialistic, and share some of my father's objections to consumerism. I only occasionally enjoy shopping. I appreciate good design, but I don't think I am remotely interested in material goods as status symbols. Big ticket designer labels and luxury car adverts leave me cold.

I want a sustainable balance, the holy grail of the self-employed. In terms of spending, I am talking about being content and generous of spirit, with myself and others, rather than worried and tight. It's not about suddenly wanting to buy loads of stuff.

I've found Helen's comment about spending and investment very helpful. She wasn't talking about the stock market or becoming a property magnate. She meant investing in a wide variety of ways that imply an emotional rather than simply financial future return. Applying this in my life is about understanding what I am buying and why I am buying it. It is a calmer and more considered approach to deciding what to spend on than my habitual tactics.

I have always relied upon an instinctive balancing of the earning and spending equation, for my personal financial management. A *feeling* of being flush or skint. Lock down interspersed with occasional sprees. Uncontrolled spending on the 'allowed' things and none on the 'not allowed'.

The irony that I, as a former chartered accountant, am only now discovering the usefulness of budgeting is not lost on me. But I have started setting budgets for the areas I have struggled with, like clothes or holiday spending. It doesn't come naturally but what it means is that I probably spend less – or at least no more – overall. I am slowly becoming more steady and mindful about each transaction. Of late I feel calmer, less guilty or worried. It even makes it easier to *not* spend on something if it takes me beyond the budget rather than resentfully turning away from whatever it is.

I still have a long way to go. But the conversations have helped me to reflect on the impact of my habitual way of managing my own earnings and spending on myself. Whilst it is not all bad and has served me successfully so far, it is benefiting from some adjustment.

This is more significant than I'd ever expected when I set out on this project. I hadn't realised that my relationship with money was a factor that could get in the way of me becoming the older woman that I would ideally like to be. To be the outward-facing, productive, helpful, interesting, convivial, creative, supportive person I aspire to be, I need a slightly different approach to money, both earned and spent. Thanks to the conversations, I'm developing some ideas about how to do that. It's still work in progress.

Managing

It was a struggle financially when we were bringing up the children. But out of that comes resourcefulness, unless you want to sink. And through being resourceful, you have a sense of achievement.
—Cecelia

I manage the household budget. I make everybody laugh because I write every single household transaction down. I've always done it. I know exactly where we are, so I know when I can say, let's go a bit wilder.
—Kate

At one time, we had about one and nine to live on. When I went to the shop I thought, do I need it? No. Put it back. We were very careful, both of us. We got through it and recovered, but it wasn't a nice time.
—Tanje

Managing the household budget is often something that falls to women. My mother is fantastic at it – she is of the same school of thought and action as Kate – whilst I am in something more akin to the second division. It seems to work.

I have had phases where I've had to put things back in the supermarket. I know how to cook lentils and fortunately we all like them. I am voucher queen when it comes to our local supermarket (which of late has gone overboard so that it feels as if you're being given sheaves of homework in addition to simply buying some food). I'm a big fan of our local greengrocer and am always amazed by how much you can buy for a tenner if you stick to what's in season.

Personally, I agree with Cecelia that there is a certain satisfaction to be gained from being resourceful. It puts me in mind of what I observed in the trip to Cuba that I mentioned earlier. The Cuban people, through long necessity, must be amongst the most resourceful in the world. It is inspiring. *Nothing* is wasted. Every family seems to have at least one master (or mistress) of invention in residence. Some of the homes we visited were overflowing with Heath Robinson style solutions to problems.

I also think that the experience of dealing with some leaner periods in life leads to a real appreciation of money when and if you do have any. Learning to live within your means – whatever they are – is a skill not always easy to acquire or maintain, especially in the complicated world of direct debits, credit cards, loans and mystifying mortgage arrangements.

My women and I grew up in times when bills were more transparent. You were invoiced for what gas or electricity or phone calls you'd used, from one supplier of each. I didn't have a credit card until I was well into my twenties with a full time job. The internet didn't get going until a good decade later, so on-line payments and one-click ordering were still the stuff of science fiction.

There was inevitably a fair amount of reminiscing when the conversations turned to managing household budgets. But I think what I have taken from this is that – whilst I don't subscribe to a 'good old days' view – there is something to be said for keeping things relatively simple. It's what I've always tried to do with the household management because – quite frankly – I cannot be bothered to juggle multiple accounts and credit or store cards or keep switching suppliers and so on.

The conversations have reinforced that view. There is a real value in doing an occasional review of what to buy from where and perhaps checking out the competition from time to time - fuel suppliers and insurance for instance. But it is always a question of weighing up the time involved against the actual money saved. There is always the issue of whether you could be doing something potentially more productive, or even lucrative, with that time. It's an on-going balancing act.

Keeping things simple in day to day management terms is a priority for me and will continue to be so. I confirmed the value in that approach from listening to these women. Having a system that works for you seems to pay off. It frees you up to think about other more interesting things.

The tricky part is developing your own system. I suspect that this is harder to do than ever for young people starting out now, as it seems to be nothing like as straightforward as withdrawing your week's cash from the bank on a Monday and living with it (the 'when it's gone, it's gone' school of financial management). Having started with that system as a young adult myself, I find I don't want to stray too far from it. Whilst I want our money managed, there's only so much time I want to devote to that process.

Independence

He's always said, we're a partnership, it's as much your money as mine – but it doesn't sort of feel like it somehow. Whereas if you actually get a salary cheque with your name on it...
—Margaret

When the children were young, I wanted to be a full time mum. I didn't have that when I was a child. That value was more important than how much money we had.
—Madeline

My mum was always cross about my dad's decision to stop paying into a pension. Her savings were very important to her. It was her version of financial independence. I don't quite feel that in the same way.
—Lesley

How money is dealt with in a relationship is an intriguing minefield. It's so rarely talked about. I know very little about how even my closest friends manage this. Joint accounts or not? Equal income or not? Household versus personal spending? Whose money is used to buy gifts for each other?

My experience has been all over the place since I became an adult. I have had years where I earned more than my husband. I have had years where I've earned almost nothing. I have had spells of being financially dependent and other times when I've been the breadwinner. I don't think I'm particularly unusual.

All these changes in circumstances mean that there is some serious scope for disagreement, resentment and misunderstanding. Power in a relationship can be wielded through money and how it is (or isn't) shared. It's a significant negotiation in any long term relationship. I came away with a strong sense of how worthwhile it is to be on the same page about current priorities in a family or partnership, and how that plays out financially. I don't think there is one arrangement that is inherently better than any other. The most important aspect is the shared understanding and agreement. I think it can take some fundamental work to get to that point.

Most of us are doing this in the dark I feel. There seems to be remarkably little advice or discussion about how to do this with a new partner, or with an existing one when circumstances change. From the outside, it is usually impossible to tell how other people do this. We make judgements on others' lifestyles without having any idea what's going on behind the scenes – debt, income, savings or pensions, windfalls or inheritances, attitudes to giving money away, supporting other members of the family, secret vices, priorities and so on.

The key, for many of the women, was about communication, trust and negotiation. It is about understanding how you *both* feel about financial independence and how that can be incorporated into a life-time shared with someone else. It probably needs reviewing from time to time as circumstances change. The message I repeatedly received was to keep talking. Keep trying.

I'm amazed really that anyone succeeds in this area. There are so many potential areas for disagreement. However, I was encouraged that, by and large, the women I listened to had all reached workable financial arrangements with their partners. Over time they've found ways that work in their situation, and ways of tolerating or living with some of the differences that may exist between them. It *is* possible, though it seems really quite remarkable.

Pensions

There are a lot of pressures. It is an era of, why didn't you provide for yourself? As a woman. You know, what were you thinking?
—Lesley

I have one word to say about pensions. AAAARRRGGGHHH.

We are all subject to the prevailing economic conditions that we are born into. The relatively short historical period of generous pensions is over. Most people of my age and younger are having to adapt to the idea of working longer for a smaller annuity. I have very little pension provision in my own name. This is not through recklessness or from not understanding the importance of saving for older age. I've contributed to whatever arrangements I've been offered. But self-employment and parenthood do not tend to leave much spare to invest.

It is highly unlikely that I can make up for that in the fifteen remaining years before conventional retirement age. We live in hope that we can live off whatever pension my husband will get (which is by no means guaranteed even though it is as good as it gets in terms of a current conventional company scheme), and I expect to carry on working well past my mid-sixties. I am lucky that I have the kind of work that might mean I am able to, and indeed that I want to. I simply can't think of anything else to do.

This is one of the few areas where I felt that the conversations could not reassure or teach me much. I am younger than these women. I probably won't get anything like the same pension provision, either alone or with my husband. We're going to have to be creative, lucky or both. That's going to need resilience and energy, and a good understanding of my overall relationship with money – all of which the conversations have helped with.

How much is enough?

There's so much stuff today, that you think, actually do I really need that? No. My sister taught me this – there can be great fun in making do.
—Liberty

We didn't have much money but we had a really good radio, good books, an oilcloth on the table and flowers on it. And that's it. What more do you need in life?
—Cecelia

I was desperately hard up in my twenties. I swore I'd never go to that borderline existence again. But now I have the

freedom – and at the same time, the problem – of having
money. Because what is enough? What do you need? No idea.
If you knew it would be fine.
—Marie

The research shows[4] that happiness is linked to having a modest income (enough to lift you out of poverty) but that beyond that, there is a law of diminishing returns. Our own perceptions of how much is enough can be deceptive, leading us to feel as if we are trying to pin down a rainbow or mirage. It can be a lifelong and somewhat fruitless chase for some people.

Poverty should never be romanticised. Being cold and hungry is never enjoyable. But above that, how much money is enough?

What I gleaned from the conversations was the value of contentment. It can be elusive. It means not focusing on direct comparison with our peer group. It means having trust that somehow things will turn out however they turn out, without having to shore up our insecurities about the future with ever-increasing bank balances. It means making the effort to notice or enjoy some of the free things in life and it means not measuring everything in financial terms.

Interestingly, I remember an evening spent with friends of friends who – we had been reliably told – were considerably wealthier than we are. This proved to be the case. They kept telling us. All I can remember about the evening is that every comment they made – about *anything* – came with a price tag. How much had been spent on the toddler's outfit, how much the bottle of wine cost, how much they needed to insure their jewellery for. It was striking. It came across as a stressful way of living to me. It appeared that nothing happened in their lives that was not somehow evaluated in financial terms. I am quite sure they did have a much higher bank balance than us, but we didn't want to swap places. Life seemed to be passing them by, whilst they counted the cost.

I am also aware of sad cases of people who have saved throughout their life to put as much as possible aside for a feared older age. They have denied themselves heating, holidays, and enjoyable times with friends and family, in the pursuit of this illusion of safety. Sometimes people in this mindset can end up leaving far more money than they might have realised or intended to their relatives or other beneficiaries. The rainy day never came, or it was completely different from what they'd feared when it did. I am not saying that there is no point in saving for the future, but money can't buy certainty. It doesn't seem wise to put myself into deliberate poverty now to try to avert poverty later. There has to be a balance. It's a difficult judgement to make.

And this was the lesson from the conversations I think. It was about maintaining a lively awareness of the very many aspects of life that money can't buy, or can only partially contribute towards. Friendship, love, cast-iron security, or certainty. It can't guarantee good health or happiness. It can't make the sun shine or the rain fall.

Money *can* make our lives more comfortable and it can enable us to do things that we otherwise wouldn't be able to. Not living in poverty makes a huge difference to our chances of living to a healthy old age. Money is undoubtedly important in the culture we live in. But we all have to draw a line somewhere about what we feel is enough and this seems to entail a degree of faith in our own resourcefulness and luck. It is not possible, or sensible, to try to provide for every possible calamity.

The discussion of money was one of the most interesting areas of the conversations for me, unexpectedly so. Like appearance, I found that money was, in different ways, simultaneously more *and* less important than I'd previously thought. The inner hippie of course is delighted that not everything is about money, and if it was we'd be in danger of missing the point in many fundamental parts of life.

But the outer middle-aged woman, parent and business-owner lives in a world where money cannot be ignored. It therefore feels more important than I'd realised to examine my relationship with it, and what it means in terms of enabling or preventing me from living in the way that I hope to in the years to come.

....

WHAT MATTERS

- Not being in poverty
- Being paid fairly
- Understanding our personal history and relationship with money
- Reviewing and challenging our monetary habits

WHAT DOESN'T

- Believing money can keep us totally safe
- Trying to define how much is enough
- Having conflicted emotions about money (it comes with the territory)
- Trying to transcend or ignore money (fantasy land)

CHAPTER 9

TONIC

A dose of reality – dwelling on it – cartwheels –
taking care – menopause – how are you in yourself? –
what matters – what doesn't

Figures released by the Office for National Statistics in 2012 suggest that for women born in the UK today, life expectancy is 82 years and healthy life expectancy is nearly 66 years. For those who have already reached 65, life expectancy is another 20 years, with healthy life expectancy being just over 11 years. It's the gap between the life expectancy and the *healthy* life expectancy that grabs my attention. For girls born today that is sixteen years, or one-quarter of their adult life. That's a long time to not be, or feel, in good health.

Asked what the worst thing about growing older is, nearly all of the women answered 'health'. The actual or feared loss of health looms large. Understandably.

Many of the women have experience of some serious health problems. Between them, they have had, or do have, Parkinson's, fibromyalgia, cancer, arthritis, osteoporosis, hip replacements, allergies, asthma, mental health issues, atrial fibrillation and probably more that we didn't talk about. Some have had life-threatening accidents.

By contrast, I have been extremely fortunate so far with my

own health. I was interested in how these women dealt with ill-health when it happened, and how they looked after themselves to try to prevent poor health, and to boost their energy and well-being. I am also always interested in the connection between physical and mental health.

What I was especially struck by was that, although I was aware of significant health issues for a fair number of these women, I came away from every conversation feeling energised, upbeat and positive. Despite the reality of health issues they described, and despite very real fears about them, what I saw and heard was all about interesting lives being lived alongside managing any illness or disability. Whilst none of them would wish to have the conditions they may have, they did not seem to be completely floored by them.

This is a difficult topic. It's not one that many of us take lightly. It's one that most of us fear at some level. Ill-health is often strongly associated with ageing in our minds. I was nervous – was this going to be a depressing discussion of inevitable and painful decline? At the same time, it felt like an important subject to cover.

A dose of reality

I had oesophageal cancer, fourteen years ago, and I believe I was very fortunate. I recovered. We're going to a funeral on Friday, of someone who didn't.
—Kitty

I had a pretty devastating breakdown. I was hospitalised for a week, and then on anti-depressants for three years.
—Liberty

Although I wish I hadn't got Parkinson's, and atrial fibrillation, and sleep apnoea it could be worse. At least I'm not in pain. It's not life threatening, other than everything will be life threatening at some point. Life is life threatening in the end!
—Margaret

The illness I heard about was not all related to age. Some is. But actually, when I listen to the recorded conversations again, I noticed that the serious illnesses and conditions that have occurred have happened at a variety of times throughout these women's lives. There is clearly a correlation between getting older and some extra aches and pains, and the longer you live, the more chance there is of contracting *something*. It is also clear that the onset of some conditions tend to occur in later life. But in my sample of twenty, the link between illness and age wasn't quite as we might imagine, and age wasn't the only factor. Perhaps older age doesn't inevitably follow the pattern that we might fear, in terms of health. The national descriptive statistics are not a prediction for any one of us as an individual.

For the women who had, or are, experiencing ill-health, they clearly all wished they weren't. I wish they weren't. I did not get an impression that this was easy or desirable in any way. What I did get, however, is a sense that the more they were able to face and accept what was happening, whilst at the same time not losing hope or determination to continue living life to the full, the more at peace with it they seemed to be. The acceptance led them to adapt behaviour or seek the medical help or social support they need, and the hope and determination kept a perspective that didn't allow the illness to overshadow everything.

I was also struck by the way in which the women who were experiencing the potentially most devastating conditions were quick to count their blessings. This all added to what seemed like a helpful perspective, although I do not imagine for one moment that they feel like this all of the time. It's hard – heartbreakingly hard sometimes.

I came away with a sense that it is important to face up to actual, real health difficulties. To understand what you are dealing with, and bring it out into the daylight to see what you are up against. It is important to seek appropriate help in doing that, and to ask for the support you need to make decisions about what to do next. This takes no small amount of courage.

Dwelling on it

Our friends came to visit. We've all got health issues which we discuss. After a while, I said right, we're not going mention it for the rest of the weekend. You do have to rise above it, otherwise it can pull you down.
—Tanje

What happens if one of you has dementia and you have to cope, or one of you has a stroke? I think in a way you can't worry too much because if it comes you just have to deal with it.
—Christine

Dealing with actual and real ill-health is hard enough, but dealing with our fears can be even harder in some ways. We can easily magnify what we are experiencing by focusing on it to the exclusion of other things.

I remember someone telling me about their terminally ill dog, who was going to be put down within the next couple of weeks. For a brief period just before this, the dog seemed to rally. The family went out for the day to the countryside with her. She seemed happy. A few days later, the end came as they had known it would. The owner reflected that in many ways the dog was fortunate because in the days when she felt a bit better, she simply felt a bit better. As far as we know, animals are not able to worry about what might happen like humans are. For a human in a similar situation, we would all be on high alert about what was probably coming and inevitably distressed and worried.

We can't switch off our ability to imagine what lies ahead. But sometimes our facility to do that goes into overdrive and we can depress and terrify ourselves, and each other, with worst case scenarios. The conversations showed me that finding ways to limit this is a good strategy. The more we can restrict ourselves to dealing with the *actual* things in front of us rather than agonising over the *what ifs*, the happier we seem to be, and the more energy and resilience we have at our disposal when we need it most.

Practices like mindfulness have been shown to be effective (this helps me), and for some people, a religious faith can help them. It can also be very useful to have an awareness of the balance between time spent dwelling on health problems (whether real or feared), and time spent doing other things. The other things might include spending time with other people, hobbies, and exercise - anything in fact. It relates to Tanje's conscious decision to limit discussion of health worries with her friends. Whilst the social support we offer to each other can be invaluable, sometimes that comes in the form of helping each other to build new perspectives. That may be best facilitated by having a firm agreement about when and how to focus on problems – and when and how not to.

I have known some people employ tactics to give themselves a conscious 'worry slot' at some point during the day. This means literally putting a timer on for five or ten minutes. That is the time when you can worry to your heart's content (out loud or privately). The deal is that when the timer goes off, that's it. No more discussion of, or thinking about, the issue for the rest of the day.

This is not a one size fits all approach. We are all different and one person's successful strategy might be someone else's least useful technique. However, anything that can assist us not to dwell excessively on problems, real or feared, is usually helpful. Rumination is known to magnify our anxieties, and potentially pull us down, in a uniquely human way.

The conversations were helpful in highlighting this. Most of the women seemed to have successful ways of focusing their attention on the positive, as well as distracting themselves, when they faced situations they could do little about. It didn't mean they never worried or got anxious, of course. But it did come across as a healthy take on what life threw at them.

Cartwheels

My illness was diagnosed when I was in my mid-forties. The consultant warned me that there is no cure and I could be in a wheelchair by sixty. Years later, when I was really unwell, my family doctor asked what the self-help group thought. I didn't know there was one.

It was held in the same building where I'd been diagnosed, but I wasn't told about it at the time. The people I have met have enabled me to overcome the symptoms. I can't get rid of the condition, but I can learn to live without all of the symptoms. The medical profession is not taking this on board.

Now I am in my sixties, I want to go back to that doctor and do a cartwheel in his office. Tell him not to tell anyone else that there's no way out of this. Please listen to the possibilities.

—Helen

For me, this story highlighted the mysterious link between mind and body. Our expectations and what we believe (often based on what we are told) are powerful. Meeting the right people to support and encourage us and perhaps introduce us to new and helpful strategies can make a huge difference. These people may be healthcare professionals, or other people who share the same conditions. It could be anyone of course.

It is a story of not giving up. Being told that there is an inevitable downward trajectory to a condition by someone in authority can become self-fulfilling. I am not naïve. I do not think it is possible to overcome anything just by wanting to. We all need to find a balance between what is within our control and what isn't, and in my opinion, it would be a foolish person who didn't at least listen to what doctors can tell us about our symptoms and conditions.

But whether it comes from a medical source or elsewhere, it seems wise to seek out safe ways of restoring our hope (without causing extra harm). Individual doctors and nurses can be good, or not, at this. Self-help groups vary immensely. There are a wide variety of charitable support organisations for different conditions and populations. These may not be for everyone, but they seem worth exploring.

For me personally, I come from a relatively sceptical scientific background and there are many alternative therapies that I would not place my faith in. I feel that we need to keep our eyes open when deciding what to do, and especially what to spend our money on. But I also think that our beliefs are enormously powerful in assisting (or hindering) our behaviour and outcomes. The placebo effect is not to be sniffed at. Our beliefs can engender optimism which can lead to behaviour and attitudes which are the opposite of giving up. And that can lead to all sorts of unexpected outcomes.

In Helen's case, being told the situation was likely to be hopeless was not helpful. I actually doubt that is ever helpful even when the physical facts may look pretty dire. There is a difference between acknowledging and accepting that there is a problem to deal with, and predicting a definite course of events. I can't comment on how individual doctors, or the profession as a whole, communicate to patients the likely progress of their illness. But if – knowingly or not – it comes across as taking all hope away, I can't see how that can assist in managing any illness.

In Helen's case, she discovered a new source of support and practical help which she didn't know existed. Her hope and belief that she could feel better was boosted. This has led to a series of events that have resulted in her *actually* feeling much better. She is not in denial about having her illness. She has to make a number of adjustments to accommodate it. But, approaching her mid-sixties, she still feels like doing cartwheels. She looks very far from being confined to a wheelchair to me. The human body and mind can be full of surprises. Never say never.

Taking care

I was set back when I had a hip replacement a few years ago. I had tennis lessons when I got better. And now I'm back to what I was before. I play three or four times a week.
—Rose

I just can't stress how important eating the right foods is to me.
—Cecelia

I once went to work with 57 stitches in my jaw. I must have been mad – now I do regret that.
—Linda

The downsides of not looking after our health (smoking, drinking, bad diet, lack of exercise) are not usually primarily about a premature death. From listening to these conversations my biggest growing realisation was that good health behaviours throughout life are about being able to be active, positive, energetic and happy in later life. It's not so much about how many years are left, a figure which none of us can know, as it is about the quality of life in those years.

This is a relatively new way of looking at it for me. I find it far more motivating than any previous mindset I've tried, in terms of taking exercise or thinking about what I eat or drink. It's much more meaningful and immediate for me than contemplating life expectancy or anything to do with my appearance. These behaviours are likely to give me the option to learn to play tennis in my later years, or continue with the walking holidays that I so much enjoy now. They are likely to dictate whether I can continue to engage fully in life. Whether

I can work, and enjoy my leisure time. The conversations have only strengthened that as I sit face to face with these resilient women. The thought of the statistically average sixteen year gap between *healthy* life expectancy, and life expectancy, is usually enough for me to put on my trainers.

All of the women I listened to have plenty of get up and go, in spite of the health concerns they may have. I want to be like that.

So I've started making some small changes. As would be expected when talking to twenty women, some of them mentioned their struggles with keeping their weight down. I have had the fortunate kind of metabolism that has kept me at a fairly stable weight all my life (I know. Bully for me). However, with the onset of the menopause, I have noticed my weight gradually creeping up. We deliberately don't own any scales but my jeans don't lie. There's also an inevitable rearrangement going on with my body at this stage – parts of me are flopping and sagging and becoming rounder and more spread out and generally are less toned and elastic. It does, I tell myself slightly too often, happen to the best of us in some form or other.

However, it was only really after these conversations that it slowly dawned on me that perhaps there is some merit to keeping an eye on my weight. I've always distanced myself from that, and have never done diets. I don't think there's a lot of evidence that they work in the longer term. But prompted by my reflections, I have started doing a monthly weigh-in at my local chemist (I still don't have scales). I have introduced some small new policies. My main new approach is about not drinking sugary drinks including fruit juice, and limiting what I drink to tea, coffee, water and wine (this is no hair shirt approach). I am trying – so far with reasonable success - to limit my alcohol intake to be well within the weekly and daily recommended levels (the 'Drinkaware' website is a useful resource to check up on this).

This is a slow way of losing weight, which doesn't grab any headlines. In nearly a year I have lost about nine pounds. It seems to go up some months, down others, with apparently no real rhyme or reason. But overall, the direction has stopped being on a constant upward trajectory. I don't know how long it will last or whether I can maintain it for the years to come. The weight per se isn't the issue. It's just a reasonably useful measure to help keep myself in good form for an active older age as much as I can. There are no guarantees but it's about improving the odds.

At the same time, I am gradually introducing more exercise into my weekly routine. It's not easy to balance with everything else there is to do, but it seems to be one of the crucial elements to an active older age. Paying attention to anything that helps to maintain muscle and bone strength, as well as suppleness, is an increasingly important priority.

The other aspect that I was aware of in the interviews was the tendency for a few of the women to ignore their own health, especially when they were busy or had other responsibilities. Going to work with fifty-seven stitches was one very vivid example. None of the women recommended that even if they'd done it themselves. I have taken note. Sometimes, we need to put ourselves first.

The conversations have definitely been instrumental in changing my behaviour. It's made me *want* to do what I can in terms of health-related behaviours rather than feeling a resentful pressure about what I think I 'should' be doing. It's less of a willpower exercise than it used to be. Inspiring. I hope it lasts.

Menopause

The menopause is a funny thing, people talk about the physical effects, the HRT, the sweats and all that, but I found it's the emotional stuff that's really big.
—Anne

I don't honestly remember going through the menopause.
—Cecelia

Surprisingly on reflection, the issue of the menopause didn't come up much at all in the conversations. I am already well into it, at a relatively young age.

When I first became aware of it, I noticed the hot flushes and also various emotional and cognitive symptoms that I didn't know were part of the deal. I'd forget words half way through sentences. My moods went rather awry at times. Personally, I would recommend talking to a friendly family doctor about it, especially if you are under fifty. It's worth understanding the various implications of changing hormone levels, in relation to contraception, and health risks such as osteoporosis. This is not the same thing, to my mind, as medicalising a natural process which I was reluctant to do. But – most of us don't let nature take its course anyway. There would be many more babies around if we did.

I guess I wasn't especially interested in the topic of menopause as I've been living with it for a while. The hot flushes are an interesting phenomenon in themselves – the sudden bursting into flames was not like anything I'd experienced until I remembered labour. Hot flushes don't hurt of course. But the memory of my body doing something in an intense physical wave over which I had no control made me realise that this was all part of the same biological system. And no giggling at the back – but I reckon orgasm can go into that category too. Anyway, just a thought. I'm not claiming to be a biologist.

By and large, the menopause has so far been all right in physical terms for me, because my discussions and weighing up of risks with my doctor resulted in going along the HRT (hormone replacement therapy) route. That's a decision for every woman to take for herself.

What I have found especially interesting is the sense of upheaval that seems to come along with it. I don't know how much to attribute to the approach of my fiftieth birthday, the children approaching adulthood or a pure hormonal surge. I'll never know. But one way or another, I realise this whole project and book is part of the turmoil. It's big enough for me to want to write all this and look at all aspects of life. So in a way, this book might be all about the menopause, whilst rarely directly mentioning it.

How are you in yourself?

My husband's mum is 90 in January and she's got everything you can think of wrong with her. You still come off the phone laughing. My kids say, Nana's a tonic.
—Tanje

I've had loads of health problems. I had a terrible accident. But I've got no time for it. I think my feisty state of mind comes from the fact that I know my time is limited, therefore it's

immensely precious. I've got to be ill enough to be in bed before I'll give in.
—Liberty

As a child, hanging around bored when my mum or grandma bumped into friends and chatted over my head (for *hours* I'm sure), there was often a part of the conversation that circled around the health of mutual acquaintances. After muted references to the details (which always made me prick up my ears – there's nothing like adults lowering their tone of voice, or even better, *mouthing* words to each other, to alert a child to tune in), the question was often asked, 'But is he/she all right *in themselves?*'. All those years ago, I thought it was a ridiculous question, but now I absolutely know what it means.

It comes back to the complex balance of mental and physical health. It seems that people can cope with an astonishing level of illness or disability if they can maintain a resilience that means they are all right *in themselves*. The conversations have led me to conclude that this is the area that *may* be most within our control. Even then I think it is a slippery thing to influence. All sorts of things can lead to us feeling out of sorts, and it can be difficult to get your mojo back if you've lost it.

But the conversations, with these spirited and thoughtful women, showed the value of making an effort to be all right in ourselves. This can involve food, hobbies, creative projects, relationships, exercise, seeking the right kind of help, being kind to ourselves when we feel vulnerable, or consciously focusing on those things that make us feel stronger. Nothing can guarantee that we won't be ill, physically or mentally. But this mix of things may just help us prevent or manage illness if we have to.

There's a huge dose of luck involved. But wouldn't it be great to be described as a tonic by those two generations younger than us?

....

WHAT MATTERS

- Hope
- Nurturing good health behaviours
- Being all right in yourself
- Focusing on actual events rather than feared ones

WHAT DOESN'T

- Predicting the course of events
- Focusing on life expectancy
- Making too strong a link between health and age
- Being a hero when you feel unwell

CHAPTER 10

DOMESTIC GODDESS

Standards – the trials of Sisyphus – division of labour – priorities – what matters – what doesn't

....

When my teenagers are away, I usually have an uncharacteristic urge to clean the house. I go at it with gusto. For about two days, I'm a whirlwind of domestic virtue. Tired and happy, I then settle into a new kind of routine where things stay where I leave them. Empty surfaces aren't instantly filled with bags, shoes, homework, cast off crockery and hair accessories. Meals are an incredibly quick fix for two of us. I miss the girls, but I don't miss the volume of relentless housekeeping that any family home requires.

When I have had a major domestic offensive campaign like this, it's quite a nice change until a few days in when I realise that keeping it in a stage of relative perfection (ha!) requires more or less full time attention. *Even* with just the two of us in residence. Dust, grease, grime, fluff, fingerprints, cobwebs, crumbs, hair, empty packaging, cast off newspapers, mail, receipts, footprints, used towels, out of date food, tired fruit, abandoned flowerpots, neglected windows, sticky residues, spillages, ashen fireplaces, silted up appliances, laundry, slept in bed linen, chipped paintwork, the garden (oops, nearly forgot about that altogether) – *is there no end* to the details to be considered?

No, is the short answer. It surely feels infinite. There is *always* something else that could be done. What about the household administration and errands, for example? I haven't mentioned them – the post office trips, boiler servicing, dry cleaning, bills, school forms, birthday cards, mending.... STOP. It can *never* be declared finished. I think you could drive yourself completely insane with trying. I'm not going to risk it.

On the other hand, I don't want to live in a dysfunctional pig-sty (sorry, pigs – below the belt). I really dislike having to move things out of the way in order to serve up dinner, or eat at the table, or sit down on the sofa. I don't want to be able to eat off our kitchen floor (that's why we have plates), but I do want a sense of order and a reasonably pleasant space to relax in.

As with everything else it seems, it is about balance. But striking that balance can be difficult, especially if you live with other people. Who should be doing what? What standards should be met? How do we negotiate different standards within the same house? How the heck do you get anything else done?

Standards

Domestic work? It's never been very important – but then I can't bear it being dirty so there is a problem.
—Val

I like Quentin Crisp's idea that after the first half inch of dust you don't notice the rest of it.
—Helen

If somebody's coming – I didn't for you – but if somebody's coming, I give it a wipe over.
—Jane

As women, there is often an underlying legacy from somewhere (our own mothers or grandmothers? Etiquette? Societal or religious teachings?) which defines the 'Done Thing'. A deep sense of shame and embarrassment could strike at any moment if you were, or are, found wanting. Not many generations back in my family, my ancestors were employed in service to wealthier families. I guess they worked to hard and fast Victorian rules and standards, and were punished if they didn't meet them. There's still probably a shadow from that era hanging over many of us.

The specifics may change from generation to generation – have you scrubbed your front door step or polished your brasses recently? Or, to take a current example, when did you last clean the inside of your fridge? I realised the latter was a hot spot of shame for me when I recently saw an article about an art project where someone had – apparently unannounced – photographed the inside of people's fridges. I could feel myself blushing in horror at the very idea.

If we have people staying with us and I have forgotten to give the fridge a quick glance over, I am instantly embarrassed if I notice them innocently trying to find something like the butter for their toast. They are greeted with what *probably* isn't a health hazard but almost certainly doesn't match up to what I imagine are European Kitchen Standards. As for our oven... Enough. I don't need to wash our dirty linen in public (and that reminds me. The laundry...).

Why do *I* feel embarrassed by these things when the rest of the family is cheerfully oblivious? It's not as if we live in a dangerous hovel – honestly, I think it is generally safe to eat here – but I feel the need to apologise to witnesses and guests as if it is a reflection on me and me alone. I feel as if I have to justify *to myself*, as much as anyone else, that I am doing all sorts of other worthy things, whilst I fear that the house is deteriorating into a place beyond redemption. In actual fact, I don't think anyone else – visitors or family – really notices that much. It all seems fine, more or less. No one has ever said anything, turned their nose up or refused to come in, sit down, eat or use the facilities.

The mixture of defiance and apology comes through in the conversations too. I especially love 'if someone's coming – I didn't for you – I give it a wipe-over'. Brilliantly refreshing. I actually felt so pleased to be in someone's home (I'd never been there before) *without* her feeling the need to clean first. It felt as if it let me off the hook for any possible return visits, which leaves us free to do or talk about things way more interesting instead.

Many women are – and the conversations reflect this – incredibly quick to internalise imagined norms. Magazines, media, history, adverts and comparison with friends and neighbours, often stoke these invented standards so that we are comparing our own practice with one that doesn't really exist. It can create psychological Achilles' heels for us, based on virtually no hard information, or without a genuine problem or issue in the first place. The small voice in our heads is whispering 'What will people think?' in relation to our own particular vulnerable spots (in my case the fridge. And the oven). It seems so ultimately fruitless. Comparison gone mad.

What I took away was a wry and reassuring acknowledgement that we all seemed to be in the same boat.

Everyone I spoke to wanted their house to be clean (ish) and orderly (ish). No-one said that they enjoyed cleaning, or found it rewarding, as a regular activity. Eyes were rolled, and exasperated sighs were sighed when I brought up the topic.

I personally find that I have a few 'life is too short to....' mantras. It's generally too short to peel potatoes (they mash, roast and boil fine with the skins on), iron anything that isn't *absolutely* essential, wash the car if you can still see out of it. These have served me well on the whole, though they benefit from the odd tweak now and then.

All I can conclude is that it makes sense to make peace with our own standards, rather than feel driven by someone else's or – especially – being driven by imaginary ones, left over from previous eras or dreamt up by the marketing departments of companies who make household cleaning products. It's fine to have much higher standards than mine of course, and I can see how nice it is when I visit people who do – but this seems only worth it if you are genuinely content with the time, effort and money involved in keeping things that way.

The trials of Sisyphus

Housework is like the trials of Sisyphus, where he has to push the rock up the hill and every night it comes down again. Whatever you do, cooking, cleaning, ironing, washing, shopping, you just do it one day, and the next day – right there again.
—Helen

If you're a housewife you're always on duty. It's a job for life. You never get any promotion, you never get any paid holidays,

you don't get a Christmas bonus. It's always there.
—Margaret

One of the most helpful quotes about home-making I came
across was on a visit to Shenandoah National Park in the Blue
Ridge Mountains, USA, when we happened upon the Brown
House – the rural retreat of President Hoover and his wife, Lou,
at the Rapidan Camp. It's now a museum, but retains a lovely
sense of relaxed and simple homeliness even though it was, I
believe, the backdrop for international politics of the highest
stakes at a time of economic meltdown. My knowledge of
American political and economic history is about as hazy as it
is possible to be, but a trivial detail that I remember is that Lou
Hoover – a remarkable woman in her own right - had a saying
that 'A home is a work-in-progress'. I felt like cheering. It's been
something of a motto for me ever since. As an aside, I have to
say I hope it's just unhappy coincidence for her that her married
name became a verb for cleaning carpets.

In any case, she has allowed me to drop any foolish notions
of being able to finish the housework. Which brings us on to
the important question of who tackles this unremitting series of
domestic jobs...

Division of labour

*Actually my husband couldn't afford me if he had to pay for
it. We worked out how much it would cost if he had to pay for
everything that I did domestically.*
—Liberty

*We are an untidy family. When I was working we always had
a cleaner. I said to the whole family if they wanted their room
cleaning, they had to tidy up. That was a very bad thing to
say because then they never did anything, so it wasn't cleaned
or tidied.*
—Christine

*I do most of the cooking but my husband has learned how to
cook. At a moment's notice he can either take over the meal or
he can cook it from scratch. So he's a good cook now but I still
do the bulk of it, probably because I like it.*
—Nicole

Household management is an interesting area in terms of
division of labour. The underlying truth in our house seems to
be that none of us particularly enjoy the jobs that are required
to keep the house ticking over in a functional way. We all have
some chores that we do as a matter of course, and some that we
avoid at almost all costs. I think we would all be happy to let
someone else do the cleaning and a lot of the tidying.

None of us relish the occasional maintenance jobs (the
filters in the dishwasher, the grout in the bathroom, the gutters,
cleaning out the freezer – although I do accept that there can be
a ridiculously colossal satisfaction on the completion of these
oft-postponed activities). We've all got what we think are better
things to do. So then it becomes an issue of who cracks first. Or
who's most successful at nagging, or persuading.

Nowhere was this more apparent than when I lived in shared
student houses. Standards always sank to those of the most
tolerant person, unless the less easy-going inhabitants caved
in and cleared it up. There was always a risk that the person

who could hold out the longest would never really have to pull their weight if other people got there first. That wasn't fair so it rationally followed that we all got pretty good at sitting on our hands. And therefore the house was in a disastrous state most of the time. They were formative years.

In a family setting, this is complicated because the adults have more responsibility for the house than the children. Custom and practice grow up about gender and adult/child roles at the same time as the children grow up. Add in the embarrassment factor that seems to be a particularly female trait in my experience, and the scene is set for the woman to be the one who concedes first, or feels most responsible. She develops ways of tackling certain tasks, and becomes skilled at them. My personal experience is that it can then be hard to watch someone else doing them badly or differently from us, and the temptation is to take over. Bingo. Fully-fledged domestic goddess – or, arguably more accurately, domestic martyr.

In a family too, the standards are highly unlikely to be the same amongst everyone in the household. My children can, and do, see to their own laundry at times, but often they are content to leave it hanging around for days on the clothes-horse, and then just take off items as they want to wear them. I think they genuinely can't see it cluttering up our shared space. Worse, they very occasionally wash a particular outfit that they want to wear and instantly transfer it to the drier because they want it *right now.*

Meanwhile, as controller of the household bills, I shudder at the idea of the electricity used to dry sopping wet clothes direct from the washing machine. On the other hand, I can remember dealing with my laundry in a very similar way as a young woman. What was the point of making an effort to put it away as I was only going to wear it again?

But now, as an adult in a house I want to relax in, I really don't want damp, or already dry, clothes hanging around for longer than necessary. The probable crux of the matter is the generational difference in our approach to leisure time. We, no doubt regarded as the grumpy old man and woman of the house, often choose to spend more of our time off at home than our teenagers do. We like our home. We relish evenings in far more than we did thirty years ago. But in practice, this often means we are staying at home with the kids' laundry for company.

So what happens? I either nag them to do it (which might be successful but involves staying on the case, and thinking about it much more than I want to), or I resignedly sort it out myself. For my husband, cups and plates left around, shoes and bags all over the place, and DVD's left out of their boxes, are other particular bug-bears that can drive him to distraction. He's left with the same dilemma.

I am absolutely sure there are versions of exactly the same scenario going on in every family home. I don't know anyone who claims to have solved it. Harmony relies on a sometimes uncomfortable trade-off, as far as I can make out. For every irritating habit members of my family have, there is another one that compensates. The laundry and crockery, for instance, can be a flash point, but at other times, my children cook dinner, bake fabulous cakes, or make jam. They are willing, welcome and capable members of the team at times like Christmas. It's not all bad by a long way.

I gave up trying to tidy or clean the children's rooms ages ago – and most of the time the rooms look as if they are in a state of crisis to my adult eyes. But now and then I am suddenly aware of the vacuum cleaner going and bags of rubbish being taken out, and I think that my laissez-faire approach may be having some kind of impact. They are – spasmodically – learning to take responsibility for their own space. It's a step further with regard for the shared rooms I suspect, especially when that is mixed with trying to become independent of your parents. To be fair, I didn't 'get' that until I had moved out of my parents' house. I've decided to draw a veil over what my mother used to say about my bedroom when I was a teenager.

The conversations reflected the constant balancing act that housekeeping requires. Weighing up whether to pay someone else to do some domestic jobs (like cleaning – we don't currently have a cleaner, but we have in the past and might do so again), how to divide the chores and responsibilities between members of the household, and how to reconcile the irritations that are inherent with sharing space, are ever-present challenges. Lou Hoover was right. It really is work-in-progress.

Priorities

Of all the domestic tasks I think cooking matters the most, because it allows people to come together and can be enjoyable for everybody. I think cooking matters more than cleanliness.
—Nicole

I do more cooking, I wouldn't say I do it all. I could get worked up about it but that's not the battle I'm going to fight. When I come home, he might have tidied up some days if he feels like it, but I'm not that fussed about that. Food, I want food.
—Lesley

I enjoyed the gardening and the cooking – it was only housework I didn't like.
—Margaret

In our house, I do most of the cooking – partly because I have an interest in food and nutrition, and, probably more significantly, I have an extremely good appetite. I have mental guidelines about eating seasonally, not wasting food, making the most of special offers, making sure we eat lots of vegetables (because I love them, it's just a bonus that they are good for you), having at least one or two meals a week with fish, not eating meat every day and so on.

It sounds rather puritanical when I write it down. But it has evolved over the years and it means – selfishly really, but I think the rest of the family benefits – that I eat what I want to most of the time. I am the sort of person who still cooks even when I am alone. I have been known to make a full roast dinner for one.

Having said that, the apparently endless catering that feeding a growing family can entail does sometimes wear me down. Extra variables are thrown in, on top of my mental guidelines. How many people will be in for each meal and when will they be home? Who needs to eat early in order to go out again? Who will be home late? This has very occasionally led to the infuriating situation where I find myself cooking exactly the same meal twice in one evening. That can't be right. At that point I usually announce that 'The Kitchen Is Closed!' until further notice.

I do these week-in, week-out calculations about what to buy and cook half unconsciously. It makes it very difficult to tell someone else what to do or how to do it. I care what everyone eats in terms of nutritional balance. It's still greatly pleasing to my occasional earth mother identity to cook a nourishing meal and see empty plates all round at the end of it.

I am delighted that the children are good cooks too, although I wouldn't expect them to do the whole weekly balancing act that I do. There's cooking, and there's kitchen and household management. They are different things.

There was a consistent theme running throughout the conversations on this topic that food and cooking (for some, including the growing of food) were the key domestic priorities. I've always felt like that too.

With a good meal in prospect, or behind us, most of the other stuff feels more manageable. Good food implies a functional level of household management too – it's not possible to produce much in the way of regular satisfactory meals if the kitchen and house is in chaos. For me, this priority somehow summarises the whole contentious issue of domesticity. If there is dinner on the table, something must be working. It's not about being a goddess.

WHAT MATTERS

- Food and meal times
- Recognising trade-offs
- Identifying and accepting our own standards
- Remembering a home is a work-in-progress

WHAT DOESN'T

- Internalised norms
- Feeling solely responsible
- Whether you peel potatoes
- Trying to finish the housework. It's impossible.

CHAPTER 11

THE SOCIAL NETWORK

Beginnings, endings and realisations – thick and thin – a friend in need – being a friend – legacy – what matters – what doesn't

The rain battered down whilst we huddled over burgers and tried to avoid the cold water pouring off the tarpaulin hastily thrown across a frame above us. Wine was poured into plastic cups and shared around. Hot drinks were in high demand. Children – undaunted by the weather – tore around the playground, only occasionally returning to their parents for more food or to seek arbitration for some local dispute. The summer term was coming to an end.

By slow degrees, we noticed that the rain was easing. The evening sunlight struggled through the clouds, gradually gaining the confidence to shine as if it had meant to be there all along. Steam started to rise from the paving slabs. More people arrived. We took off our coats.

The strains of a cover version of 'Brown-eyed girl' drifted out from the school hall. Adults and children alike got up to dance. Encouraged, the band – consisting of head teacher, deputy head and parents – got louder. More people arrived, nearly everyone on foot. They had various connections with the school – past and present pupils, parents, step-parents, grandparents, staff, governors, volunteers. Children took advantage of the unusually light supervision and took off to the wild area at the back of the school field. A blast of 'Delilah' (eat your heart out, Tom Jones) rounded off the celebrations.

Later, some of us possibly a little tipsy, we gradually made our way home through the dark and quiet streets. Another school year older.

There was nothing extraordinary about the evening. It was makeshift, homemade, cheap, on the doorstep, and for all age groups. At the same time, that evening, and others like it, have always seemed to me to be the very stuff of life. It was an annual event at my daughters' primary school. We all loved it. I think it is hard to overrate the importance of community, and of friends and family.

Out of evenings like these come strong friendships, working relationships and a shared commitment to each other, as well as the vital chance for everyone to let their hair down once in a while. Evenings like this helped to weave a strong web of dependable connections. Strong enough for the whole community to pull together, not long after that evening, when the head teacher was suddenly taken ill and died in the depths of the winter. Where would we be without this social support, in good times and bad?

Recognition of the importance of this came through in the conversations. Very often women quietly hold whole communities together, and many of the women I listened to actively do just that. I didn't need convincing of the value of a strong social network. But I was very interested to hear what they had to say about it.

Beginnings, endings and realisations

When we lived in Madrid, I felt extremely lonely. One day, in the launderette, I overheard a woman speaking English. We got chatting, and she invited me to a Tupperware party. Well, to be honest, I could have sold Tupperware to her, I had so much already, but I was so pleased to be asked. Just last weekend two of the people I met there, about forty years ago, came to visit us.
—Tanje

I'm glad I went to live in New Zealand for a while. The intention was to emigrate. But until I went I didn't know it mattered to me to be in the heart of my family. It was fantastic learning.
—Marie

The expat lifestyle has given me a freedom but the constant goodbyes are restricting. I'm beginning to build my friendships again now I'm moving back to the Netherlands. I didn't realise I was doing it but I haven't let people get close to me here in the UK. As I go into this new phase of my life I need my friendships. I need to meet people spontaneously for coffee and that kind of thing.
—Madeline

I am in a generation that sometimes refers to friends as 'the new family' (I blame American sitcoms for the terminology). Many of my contemporaries left their home towns for university and work and, through necessity, have built up a strong circle of friends which have, to some extent, taken the place of family. I haven't lived near any of my relatives since I was eighteen and can't imagine what it would be like to pop round during the week or come across them whilst shopping. I can just about get to my parents and back in a day but it's a three hour drive away so usually it means at least a weekend visit. My brother lives on the other side of the world, in New Zealand.

On one memorable occasion, we did bump into my (only) cousin and her family when we were on holiday in Cornwall, and I think my daughters are, to this day, embarrassed about how loudly I yelled and how excitedly I leapt over chairs and tables in the café to get to them. If I unexpectedly bumped into my brother, I would be so surprised that my shrieks would be heard for miles.

Despite not growing up where I now live, I feel a very strong sense of community. I encounter people I know just about every time I step out of the door or into the supermarket. None of this takes away from the importance I attach to my family. It's just that I need friends as well – and so do my relations. Making friends as we get older isn't always very easy. Children can help to lead the way into a community, but with or without that, it can be about making a conscious effort to approach people, take up new interests, and to risk trying to develop friendship further.

Several of the women I listened to have experience of moving around internationally. It seemed to me that this brought into sharp relief what they needed, or may unexpectedly have led to a realisation of what they have been missing, in terms of a social network. It was an interesting clarity and perspective to listen to.

It has sometimes meant they have changed plans or done things that feel somewhat artificial. Climbing over your own personal mountain of Tupperware to go to another party and buy more, for instance, may seem less than logical. However, it can serve a purpose. Aside from the plastic bowls, such events are a vehicle for making and strengthening friendships. As is any other group that we join – a choir or a quiz team, a netball club or a steel band.

We vary in our personalities and how much contact we need with other people. I dare say for some people reading this, the very idea of joining groups gives them the heebie-jeebies. These are not, of course, the only ways of meeting people, and equally, we are all different in whether we want a large circle of friends or close friendships with a very select few.

What I heard in the conversations were not prescriptive ideas of how we should go about developing our social circle, or what form this should take. It was more about appreciation and enjoyment of connection and community, whatever shape it is. This was sometimes especially clear for those who had looked at it from a distance.

Fostering and maintaining a strong social network sometimes entails some conscious management of beginnings and endings. When we are busy with work and other responsibilities it can be easy not to notice the endings, and not to work at the beginnings in the way that we might have done at other times in our lives. The conversations were a good reminder not to take our friendships – or our families or wider community – for granted.

Thick and thin

The more people who have known you over the past, the more anchored you feel. The analogy I use is that it's like making a hammock. If you have a good mesh of different friends, some from very long-standing relationships, you feel much better held in the hammock.
—Nicole

When I was sixty I decided that I wanted a weekend with my female friends. I got in touch with all the women that have been, in a way, my sisters through life. So there were friends from school, from university, more recent friends, and my sons' girlfriends. It felt really important. It was a good thing to do.
—Kate

My friends are really special. I have a friend who talks about how I am 'framily' because I'm a friend but I'm also important to her children. I've got friends who go back 40, 50 years, all over the world. It's hugely important. I get terribly upset if I think something's gone wrong with a friendship.
—Jane

To me, one of the loveliest things about getting older is the evolving and growing network of friends, colleagues, acquaintances and extended family. It feels to me like a long term tapestry or knitting project, with long running threads, new threads, short threads and a whole variety of colours and textures. It's not often that we stand back and look at the whole. In social terms, I think that's what happens when we celebrate birthdays or anniversaries.

I was warmed right through by the fervour with which the women talked about their friends and family. Even though these relationships hadn't always been easy, or haven't always been close, the big picture was uplifting. Whether they favoured one or two close friends, an emphasis on family, a very active community role or a massive global network didn't seem to matter. Of all the things that can help us enjoy the good times in our lives and weather the difficulties, this seems to be one of the most important components.

I am not at all surprised by this of course. Social support is vital to our well-being both physically and mentally. Loneliness is damaging (it's a very different thing from enjoying solitude). The conversations, as I expected, just confirmed that. But even so, it was really good to hear it.

A friend in need

I can't imagine not having friends. They might not be in your house every day but they are there if you really need them. If I was in a real pickle, they'd come.
—Margaret

One of my inspirations is one of my mother's friends. They had a really strong network of female friends. When her cancer came back, she went downhill very quickly. The network was so powerful in her last six months. She'd been very strong for other people over the years, but it is two way. I just thought, yeah, I'd like to have that.
—Anne

I don't know what I would have done without my friends.
—Jane

At the time that I was going through my divorce, I went with my daughters, then aged four and two, to stay with an old university friend and his wife for the weekend. Once the children were in bed, the grown-ups opened some wine and talked. My friend's opening comment has stayed with me ever since. 'Don't think you haven't been talked about' he said, with a wry smile.

It wasn't practical help (though having dinner cooked for me that evening was unbelievably welcome), and of course it didn't change the situation. I didn't care what had actually been said when I was being talked about. But it was exactly what I needed to hear at the time. My oldest friends were concerned. They hadn't forgotten about me.

I have many friends, local and more far-flung, who have been there at exactly the right time for me on various occasions. I hope I have done the same for them when they have needed it. It is often said that at times of crisis you find out who your real friends are. Support can come from unexpected directions, and usually isn't all from one person. How available they are, physically or emotionally, can depend upon what is going on in their lives at the time. We may need to ask for their help which, for many of us, is often something that we are not very comfortable with. In my experience though, it's usually worth risking it.

I think it is extraordinary how powerful the presence, and empathy, of someone else can be in times of need. What I heard from my women is that sometimes it can enable a crucial turning point in the midst of our troubles. Sometimes we don't recognise this until afterwards. Sometimes it's about offering

very practical assistance in terms of meals, or lifts, or childcare.
But very often it is about simply connecting, and caring. The
value of this should not be underestimated.

Being a friend

*I do work hard at maintaining friendships. That doesn't mean
to say I flog a dead horse. But I'm very aware that it's a two
way thing and you do have to do your part. It is an effort.*
—Tanje

*The problem is that to be a wonderful mother and wife, to have
a wonderful career or be somebody who makes a living, is that
it doesn't necessarily leave enough time for friendship. You
have to understand that you might be sort of B+ at everything
rather than A+.*
—Nicole

*I've chosen not to hold on to some friends. And I've chosen to
build new friendships around interests like my creative stuff
and drama. With a lot of my friends, we can talk at a level
that's really intimate, very meaningful and reflective. It's good.*
—Simran

Friendships don't just happen. Good family relationships don't
just happen. Community doesn't just happen. They all require
some effort.

For those who have managed to develop and maintain
friendships over decades there's a clear sense that this has
needed focus and energy. Nicole describes keeping in touch

with friends during the busy mid-life years on a 'catch as catch can' basis, meaning that just enough contact has taken place to allow for more meaningful re-ignition of old friendships once the opportunity arises. I see this as one of the major roles of Christmas card contact or, in recent years, Facebook and emails. These fleeting connections keep just enough of a thread – as well as vital practical information about contact details – to be able to pick the relationships up later.

It is interesting to reflect on what it means to *be* a friend as well as to *have* friends. The two way nature of this came across as very important. All the women recognised that for a supportive, energising and two-way connection to flourish in the long term, it is neither all about being the cheerful positive life-force the *whole time* but nor is it about being the one with the problems *all of the time* either. It's a balance, sometimes delicate, of vulnerability and support which can swing to and fro. If this equilibrium tips for too long in only one direction, it can be alienating. Being a good friend involves both being able to reveal your own vulnerabilities and worries, as well as being able to listen to someone else's.

There is a big difference between moaning and showing vulnerability. Some of the times I've felt closest to my friends have, unsurprisingly really, been when things are not going well for one or other of us. It's not a negative experience. Moaning, on the other hand, often is.

I've also noticed how some of my good friends are very skilful at asking questions. They are interested in what's going on for me. Successful long term friendships are about both parties and their needs. It can be easy to forget that when a lot is going on in your own life. We need to remember to ask others how they are – and listen to the answer. I'm sure I haven't always managed to do that.

A number of the women talked about being more selective about friendships as they got older. It sounded to me that this was about getting the balance of vulnerability and support right, for them. It involves recognising that intimacy takes effort on both sides. It also requires an awareness that their needs might change with their circumstances or age. The women have sometimes carefully considered what they feel able to offer other people, and where they want to draw boundaries. They have made decisions about how they divide their time between being with other people and having space to themselves.

This reflects something about knowing themselves well enough to understand what they can contribute to, and what they need from, their friendships. It was interesting to listen to and illustrates so clearly that there is no single model of friendship. Friendships and networks that suited one woman wouldn't have worked for another. The core elements were similar though, whatever the pattern of friendship. Relationships are two-way. And they are an investment.

Legacy

A woman who was my friend and mentor died recently, in her nineties. The extraordinary thing is that her dying has made no difference to my relationship with her. It's as if her fabulous energy, enthusiasm and sense of fun are still here. What she gave me is buried so strongly in me that the fact that she isn't here, in her body, makes no difference. What she had to give me, she gave. I've got it, and it's indestructible. It is amazing.
—Liberty

I spend quite a lot of time with my kids and my kids' partners and I love that, I find it really energising. I like being around young people.
—Kate

Some of the women talked about fear of losing their friends as they got older, and some had already experienced the death of close friends. It's a very sobering thought.

Many of my friends are the same age or older than me. We've been connected by simultaneously going through the same life stages, or by being thrown together through education, work or as a result of where we live. I fear losing them as much as anyone does.

However, I was left with two reflections from discussing this. Firstly, I felt particularly aware of the value of having a mix of friends of all ages. Many of my interests – walking, theatre and so on – mean that I often, even now, bring the average age down. I'm not sporty or musical so I don't feel that I naturally belong to groups that might entail a greater age range.

But I have realised that this is something to be gently mindful of. I'm not on a conscious mission to find younger friends, so fear not. That would be rather weird. However, when I reflect, I think it's entirely possible that I exclude myself from the younger people in a mixed age gathering, such as a conference. I may be drawn unconsciously to people of my age group or older because I feel in my comfort zone. I don't want to cramp younger people's style, and neither do I want to come across as patronising. I feel more shy around young people, than with my own or older age group, perhaps because it reminds me of the shyness I felt when I was their age.

When I consider this, I realise that I may be, completely unwittingly, perpetuating the image of older women as shadowy figures around the edges of things. This is a large helping of food for thought, which probably wouldn't have occurred to me without the conversations.

My second reflection is about the legacy left by friends who are no longer with us. I was reminded of Pam, the woman I met in Cuba. I didn't know her very well or for very long but she altered my outlook. Small things remind me of her. On one of my few visits to stay with her, she introduced my children to a whole new concept of breakfast, and I think of her every time I see them loading up a plate of steaming hot toast laden with butter, sugar and cinnamon. I hope and believe that she has passed on a little bit of her good humoured zest too.

None of us can know what we leave with other people. These twenty women have all left something of themselves with me. There are aspects of each and every one of them that spring to mind in all sorts of ways as I go about my daily life now. I suspect they always will.

WHAT MATTERS

- Making an effort to nurture friendships
- Community
- Legacy
- The two-way street

WHAT DOESN'T

- How many friends you have
- The shape of your social network
- How you make friends
- The age of your friends

CHAPTER 12

WHAT DOESN'T KILL YOU...

*Crisis – rescue – absence – resilience – expectations –
what matters – what doesn't*

....

In many ways the generation of women I have listened to –
and subsequent generations – are very lucky indeed. Whilst
many of them were born around the time of the Second World
War, they have lived their adult lives in peace in the countries
they have lived in. For me, born in 1964 in the UK, and my
contemporaries, we have lived in unprecedentedly stable times,
not that they have been without their troubles and tragedies
over the years.

In this country, we have also benefited from the National
Health Service (NHS), vaccines and antibiotics. Health and
safety legislation – whilst much pilloried – has meant that we
are far less likely to be killed or seriously injured by our work,
or other activities, than people living a couple of generations
ago. Education policy has meant that children are given a more
carefree childhood, and an opportunity to open doors, that was
not in place for many a hundred or more years ago.

This can give us a sense of safety that is partly real (in
this country and many others too, the risks to life and limb
are considerably lower than they have been at other times in
history) and partly an illusion. Interestingly, as physical risk

diminishes as a result of health advances and safety legislation and practice, it seems that psychological risk may rise, with increasing levels of depression and anxiety world-wide. I don't know whether these things are related – but it seems possible that a lower focus on simply keeping ourselves alive in the face of war, disease and dangerous work may leave us more time and energy to worry about the imponderable *what ifs*.

I have been struck as I've gone back over the conversations, how many aspects of modern life seem to involve some measure of managing fear. I've looked at it from the perspective of an ageing woman, but it applies to other groups too of course. Most of the themes the conversations covered lend themselves to worry if we let them: health, finance, children, care of our loved ones. Much of what I have heard has been about finding ways to keep those fears in a healthy perspective.

But of course, nothing can make our lives risk free. I was shocked and humbled by the accounts of crises and tragedies that a number of these women had weathered. The things that actually happened were usually completely unforeseen. None of us are immune. How did these women develop their strength to cope?

Crisis

I was flying into a remote area in the Sudan. And the plane crashed. We flipped over. I couldn't get the seatbelt undone. I couldn't breathe. I was being pushed in.
—Madeline

I met somebody that I really liked. It was really good. Then he and I and two others, a young couple, went to Italy and there

was this awful road accident. And both the men were killed.
—Cecelia

I was ironing when I suddenly noticed there was water dripping on to the shirt. I thought, what's going on? I realised I was crying. I was crying because I suddenly knew beyond all doubt that I was in the wrong place, doing the wrong thing.
—Helen

Life has dealt some devastating blows to some of the women I talked to. They are way beyond anything I have ever had to deal with. It brought home to me how fragile our existences are; how in a split second everything can change, irrevocably. Listening to these women, I wasn't sure what I could draw from these episodes in their lives. Indeed, was there anything to take away?

What I found inspiring in these painful recollections was the persistence of ordinary life in the face of the most distressing circumstances. There were examples of this in each story, however difficult. The women not only survived these events but are able to talk about them, and put them in perspective, along with many other things. They are able to laugh, drink tea, work, and plan; do far more than merely function.

They all show that life goes on. These events *are* life-changing, in ways we can't know until and unless we experience them. None of us can have an inkling of whether or when we might be thrown such an experience. I don't think any of the women I spoke to are glad that those events happened to them. But they have come to be incorporated into their life stories.

I also reflected that whilst some of these crises were random physical incidents that changed everything, such as an accident, others were crisis points in life that we may suddenly be aware of. I have some experience of the latter, which is inherent in divorce, and can also be part of other major life changes such as career change.

They are different things. Violent and dramatic accidents are arbitrary bolts out of the blue, whereas the crisis moments in life are often a result of a personal perfect storm. Different elements may have been lining up for years. We may have been dimly aware of the approaching tempest, or completely oblivious, and it takes us utterly by surprise. And at the moment it strikes – which may be just as unforeseen as an accident – we can suddenly realise that we are in the wrong place doing the wrong thing. In hindsight, it may all look a little different – we may wonder why we didn't see it coming.

Listening to these accounts, I was often in awe. Life has been extraordinarily hard at times for some of these women. Their resilience, as they sat laughing and talking about all sorts of things, had a big impact on me.

Rescue

It had been a year since my dad died and my husband left, and I cooked my daughter a meal. We sat at the table and she said to me, do you cook every day for yourself mum? And a year's worth of tears shot out.
—Linda

I finally got the seatbelt undone – and I fell. The pilot jumped out and my colleague and I were trapped. The fuel in the engine caught fire. And my husband – waiting for the plane to arrive – was the one who got me out.
—Madeline

I was too lost and too immature to know how to handle what was going on. I went to stay with my wonderful aunt in Canada who managed to give me a visualisation that took me out of that state.
—Helen

The power of other people to help us when we need it most should not be underrated. This message came through clearly and repeatedly from the conversations. Whether it is practical help, a listening ear, or someone to just be with us, the way in which this can build resilience is remarkable. It always makes me reflect again on our biological instincts. We do seem to be a very social species. We need each other for survival.

Sometimes we do simply need rescuing, in the moment of crisis. People often know what to do and are willing to do it when that moment occurs. I am writing this on the anniversary of the attacks on the World Trade Centre in New York. At the time, and in the aftermath, there were innumerable stories of rescue and connection.

Talking to these women, who've experienced traumatic moments in their lives, boosts my faith that when and if disaster strikes, someone will try to help. It's what we do for each other, and it's also what happened in the events they described.

I guess that we need to be ready to be helped though, especially in the time following a crisis. More is being learnt about post-traumatic stress all the time. It is worth seeking specialist help from those who are experienced and knowledgeable in this area, if we are experiencing severe difficulties after such an event. On a more informal level, unexpected people may turn out to be our rescuers – whether that's in the moment or over the following months and years.

Sometimes, I heard from the women that the simplest questions, or connections with people, were all it took to unlock another stage of recovery.

Absence

My mother died when I was three. At the time you don't know you're any different to anybody else, you just get on with it. In fact, I didn't even miss her I suppose till I was about 50. I realise now that throughout my life, I've missed having her as a mentor.
—Cecelia

There was one boyfriend I had when I was 17. I just wish, with hindsight, that I'd met him later. For three years we were anguished over each other. We just met at the wrong time. I wanted to spread my wings and move away and he didn't.
—Rose

I'd fallen in love with somebody. At the same time, my father had arranged a marriage for me.
—Simran

Some of the events that the women described were striking examples of the road-not-taken. We'll never know what life would have been like if this or that hadn't happened. It can be easy to fantasise about if we are unhappy with how events have actually turned out.

My father's father was 38 when he died. My father and aunt were still young children. Of course, I never met my grandfather. But I've often wondered what life would have been like for all of us, had he lived. His loss has been keenly felt, even by the generations in my family that never knew him.

My links to him have been momentary and vivid. In peace time, he made his living from a very niche business restoring chandeliers, including those now hanging in the Bath Assembly Rooms. During the war, I am told he transported Field Marshall Montgomery's tank into position for the Battle of El Alamein (apparently this resulted in personal thanks from Montgomery himself). I have seen both the chandeliers and the tank. I even sat in the tank which is still, I believe, in the entrance hall of the Imperial War Museum in London (by coincidence, I was 38 when I did that. A shiver did run down my spine). Judging by the photographs of a handsome man in uniform, which are added to many anecdotes I've heard of him, I have been left with an image of an extraordinary person. In my mind he is brave, funny, upbeat, energetic, a risk-taker, sporty, entrepreneurial, strong, kind and clever. No flaws. And forever young. A man on a pedestal, I suspect.

Absence is a powerful force. This came across as I listened to the conversations. All of the women who had experienced such absence went on to live very full lives. It didn't seem to me that they spent a lot of time pining over what might have been. They were all focused on making the most of the things and people that were present in their lives.

But I had a sense that they did just wonder what might have been, from time to time. As they talked to me, there was an air of wistfulness rather than raw pain or agonising regret. Perhaps that is the effect of time passing. Perhaps it is also a reflection of their strength of character.

My grandmother, widowed in her thirties, never really got over it. Sadly, her life – in her own eyes – became defined by absence. Even when I was a child, I think I was aware that she seemed to be looking out for loss, every time someone went away, even over short distances and for short periods of time. She struggled to focus on the very many people who were, or who could have been, present in her life. Undoubtedly, there were a whole variety of reasons for that, and perhaps she couldn't do much about them.

But what the conversations have helped me see is the value in acknowledging, but not being defined by, the absence of highly significant people in our lives. I don't suggest for one moment that this is easy.

Resilience

I think, for me, what seemed like interminable years of personal failure has led to a quite confident now. It's like I needed the bad to get to the good.
—Liberty

Later, I said, do you know what? I'm not going to be frightened of anybody any more. No one is going to tell me how to live. I am not going to be fearful, of anybody.
—Madeline

I couldn't have said this a few years ago, but now I actually believe that what's happened were the necessary pieces for me to become who I've become. What matters is that I'm at peace with it.
—Simran

Many years ago, I failed one set of my accountancy exams and had to re-sit them. Whilst this wasn't uncommon in the profession, it felt like a massive setback to me. I felt as if I'd worked my utmost and wasn't at all sure I could go through it again.

What sticks in my mind is a conversation I had on the first working day after the results were published. I wasn't keen to face everyone in the office but didn't have much choice. I bumped into one of my managers (who is now a good friend), who had also failed a set of exams some years previously. He said to me something that somehow managed to be blindingly obvious, very simple and deeply profound at the same time. He said, 'Well, there's nothing for it but to pick yourself up and do it again'. That was it. Keep going. Don't agonise, rant at the universe, or beat myself up. Just keep going.

It's stayed with me. On that occasion, I did keep going. I passed the exams the second time I sat them. I had to dig pretty deep to do that. This is clearly *nothing like* the same scale of setback or crisis that the women I've listened to have had to deal with. But the same message was inherent in their stories, even when the setbacks were far more significant than exam failure.

The women's reflections were inspiring to listen to. Getting to such a philosophical place has taken years, and a great deal of difficult experience and contemplation, for these women. I don't think that everyone can or does manage that. But it has given me confidence that it is often possible.

This state of mind is a result of a number of aspects, I think. Our personalities and support systems are important ingredients. In addition, we need to be willing to acknowledge, and accept, difficult experiences and circumstances that we can't change. This can take a long time.

Sometimes, the women made conscious decisions to alter their outlook in the future. *Deciding* not to be fearful any more, for instance, is a formidable undertaking, which often is born of the most extreme circumstances and a significant determination. We can't all find it within ourselves to do that, but I found it heartening to hear that some people have successfully taken this route.

Furthermore, the women's reflections demonstrated that our belief systems are also a very important aspect. The most significant thing that struck me was that these women didn't give up. They held on to a measure of hope and optimism. Some have a religious faith that has helped them, but many haven't. Whatever life threw at them, they kept going. It is the same message that I received from my manager.

Sometimes, I think they kept going because they simply couldn't think of an alternative. I recognise that feeling from my less extreme experiences. It can almost be calming – a sense of resignation that there is nothing to do but get through x or y. I think that is often why dealing with *actual* crises and emergencies can, unexpectedly, feel more manageable than being in a state of high anxiety about *feared* ones, where we are wrestling with imagined scenarios.

Expectations

My friend calls it the Cinderella syndrome – a belief that somehow I should just sit here, looking pretty and sweet, and everything comes to me. My prince arrives, good looking and rich, he's got the slipper and it fits.

Life's going to feel like hard work next to that. Where do we get these ideas? The reality is that everything is going to have its

dreary moments, its great moments, its rubbish moments. It's
difficult. There are no slippers.

    There is a big piece of me that still wants someone to bring
it to me on a bloody cushion.

—Marie

Managing our expectations can be like walking a tightrope.
Expect doom and disaster and we give up trying. Expect the
world to somehow deliver a ready packaged, successful future to
us, and the disappointment can finish us off when it doesn't.

How do we get the balance right? There were several
things that helped these women. Friends, family and other
people are important. So is our mindset. From the tone of the
conversations, I also think that humour plays no little role.
Another feature of my time with these women is not directly
related, but was a theme for most of them – the role of stories,
art and drama to make sense our lives. A number of the women
have developed their art and creativity, in recent years, to help
them do exactly this. Some worked in these fields all along.
Most of them read fiction and biographies, and enjoy a wide
range of film, television and drama.

And – of course – this project has meant that I have listened
hard to twenty real-life stories about getting older. They have
influenced my own views about ageing. They have raised, not
diminished, my expectations about what life might bring. There
seems to me to be scope for an optimistic view. I have heard
accounts of silver linings, coping strategies and making the most
of opportunities. More so than I used to think possible, when I
contemplated fifty and beyond.

What I've heard hasn't been sugar-coated. It hasn't
unrealistically promised some glorious middle and older age. The

women have not held back from telling me about the difficulties they have, and do, encounter. I feel as if I'm developing much steadier, more realistically optimistic, expectations than perhaps I had before I started.

Another thing that I've taken from this process wasn't explicitly talked about at all. I started this project with a sense of urgency that so often accompanies the contemplation of ageing. Time is limited, running out. It can lead to a sense that there isn't time for mistakes, set-backs or fallow periods. No time for the dreary and rubbish moments.

But as I listened, I was, counter-intuitively, impressed with how *much* time there might actually be. Not unusually, the women would describe a set-back or crisis that took a few years to process or come to terms with. They went on to do many other rewarding and productive things beyond that, and perhaps even *because* of these episodes.

There is little point – and it seems, little need – to panic. There was something strangely nurturing about the way they sometimes described being forced to slow down or put other things on hold for a while. It didn't mean they had given up. But it might have involved a change of pace or direction. Managing our expectations realistically can be both motivating and relaxing. We're less likely to take fright if it looks as if things are going awry, and less likely to give up if we don't instantly succeed.

Like most people I imagine, I still quite like the idea of success being delivered on a cushion. Perhaps this is a human desire to take the line of least resistance. But I suspect that I – and Marie – probably wouldn't enjoy it much if it was. The dreary and rubbish moments have a habit of making the great ones feel even better. And – within reason – my women's experience supports the notion that what doesn't kill you makes you stronger.

....

WHAT MATTERS

- Keeping going
- Optimism
- Help from other people
- Hindsight

WHAT DOESN'T

- Heroics
- Trying to be perfectly safe
- Slippers and cushions
- Taking time to recover

CODA
NOTES TO SELF

On a beautiful day in August, we seek out a wild swimming spot on Dartmoor. It is an idyllic setting, an ancient grassy common on the bend of the river, overhung by lush oak and beech trees in full summer leaf. Dappled sunlight falls across wet children sleek and glossy as seals, and their shrieks bounce off the rock face as they dare each other to ever higher leaps from the bank.

I bring up the rear of our little family group, as we haul our picnic and towels from the car park. My varifocals and unsteady flip flops, as well as customary caution, result in me being slower than everyone else in making my way along the uneven riverside footpath.

I imagine, if I were living in some fictional primeval tribe, that I might soon be discarded. What do I bring to the party? Am I becoming a liability? As a woman approaching fifty, I no longer offer physical strength or child-bearing potential. If I ever was physically daring, I'm less so now. The brief appeal of dipping in the river chills as quickly as my feet when I test the temperature.

I'm no longer the quickest, strongest or the one with the loudest voice. I have fulfilled my reproductive purpose, if that is what we are here for. I won't have more children and my daughters are growing in independence on a daily basis.

But I don't feel ready to resign myself to the background yet. In many ways I feel that my work has barely started. Am I deluded in thinking I have some valuable contribution to make? What shape will it take? What exactly *is* my purpose? And does it matter?

The women I have had conversations with over the last months have a wide range of views and experiences. My initial response is relief that not one of them is invisible. Their contribution may sometimes be subtle but is often all the more powerful for that.

It is like a dew-laden spider's web: visible if you look for it; awe-inspiring in its construction; efficient, beautiful and very strong in its natural habitat. It is also very easily swept aside by those clumsily making their way through life without stopping to notice what is right in front of their faces. The corporations, institutions, families and generations who ignore older women are losing far more than they realise. Society needs older women like the world needs bees.

I have heard from women, all of whom are at least sixty years old, who hold things together. They quietly and relentlessly challenge injustice. They support and soothe and organise and nurture. They lead the way. They laugh. They struggle, and doubt themselves. They keep going, and encourage others to keep going. They see the bigger picture as well as the tiny details of life that matter. They are a curious mix of astonishing patience and exasperated energy. They care.

I have paused for a while in my middle-aged rush of busy domesticity where work and motherhood uneasily co-habit, backlit in recent years by my own uncertainties about ageing. I have stopped to listen to these ordinary, yet extra-ordinary, women. I expected interesting things.

However, I didn't expect the project to be so immediately and intensely personal. It has confirmed or challenged my own views of what matters and what doesn't. It has left me with clearer ideas about the kind of older woman I would like to be. It has reassured me. It has been time well spent.

And over to you...

I hope that, by now, you are thinking about the older women in *your* life, as well as those who are in your peripheral vision, but may not have come into focus for you – yet.

I always intended this project ultimately to become a book, and that was part of the deal when I set up the conversations. However, it is, of course, possible to do a similar exercise on a much more informal basis.

If you have been inspired by what I have heard and learnt from the conversations, you could approach people you feel drawn to, inspired by, or curious about (it doesn't just have to be women, of course). Be open and clear about what you are doing. Set time aside to spend an hour or two (or three!) listening.

Ask what matters, and what doesn't. Use my questions if you want to (in the next section) or choose your own. Allow yourself time to mull over what you hear. Buy a lovely notebook. Make some of your own 'notes to self'.

Be prepared to be challenged, reassured, inspired and surprised. Be ready to come away feeling bolder – and wiser. Who knows where it might lead?

MY QUESTIONS AND APPROACH

Selecting the women

This project was not an academic one. I did not try to find a sociologically representative sample of women. I did not have a central hypothesis that I was testing. This was not a PhD.

My criteria were simple. I was looking for women who were at least sixty years old. I found them by asking friends, family, associates and colleagues and by talking about what I was doing to as many people as I could.

I decided on twenty because I felt that it was as many as I could physically manage. There is also some evidence[5,6] that this number is likely to be enough to reach saturation point, in terms of uncovering new themes.

I arranged the twenty conversations on a first come, first served basis. More women did come forward but I somewhat reluctantly decided to draw the line after the twentieth. I have absolutely no doubt that I missed some great stories and reflections by doing that, even if I was unlikely to uncover new themes. Perhaps there will be a chance to catch up one day....

It was a self-selecting group. The women who came forward had some interest in the topic and in sharing their experience with me. Some of them knew me, many didn't. The conversations were all equally interesting.

The questions

My core questions were 'what matters?' and 'what doesn't?'

I asked this in relation to work, family, marriage, friendship, health, appearance, finance, domestic work, learning and creativity. The conversations didn't have to cover all of these areas – some did, but others focused on a few of them. No-one was expected to answer anything that they didn't want to.

My other questions were intended as prompts rather than a prescriptive interview schedule. They were:

- What's the best and worst thing about getting older?
- Did you have any role models or mentors?
- Has life since you turned fifty been how you expected it to be, and in what ways (or not)?
- What would be your advice to younger women?
- What are you really glad you decided or did?
- Any regrets?
- How did you make, spot or respond to opportunities?
- What have been your most useful skills, attitudes or mindsets over the years?
- Do you have any favourite sayings or mantras that help you?
- If you were to recommend any inspirational or favourite books, what would they be?

I sent these questions to the women before we met for the conversation, and I kept a print out of them on the table between us whilst we held the conversation. It was a loose structure that helped to keep us on the subject, whilst also recognising that this topic was a very wide one indeed. There was plenty of scope for following the conversation wherever it went.

REFERENCES AND FURTHER READING

References

[1] Lyubomirsky, Sonja (2007) *The How of Happiness* Sphere

[2] Mischel, Walter; Ebbesen, Ebbe B. (October 1970) 'Attention in Delay of Gratification'. *Journal of Personality and Social Psychology* 16 (2) 329-337

and

Shoda, Yuichi; Mischel, Walter; Peake, Philip K. (1990) 'Predicting Adolescent Cognitive and Self-regulatory Competencies from Preschool Delay of Gratification: Identifying Diagnostic Conditions' *Developmental Psychology* 26 (6): 978-986

[3] Williams, M and Penman, D (2011) *Mindfulness: A Practical Guide to Finding Peace in a Frantic World* Piatkus

[4] Biswas-Diener, R and Diener, E (2008) *Happiness: Unlocking the Mysteries of Psychological Wealth* Blackwell

[5] Francis, J.J., Johnston, M., Robertson, C., Glidewell, L, Entwistle, V., Eccles, M.P., and Grimshaw, J.M. (2010). 'What is Adequate Sample Size? Operationalising Data Saturation for Theory-Based Interview Studies', Psychology and Health, 25: 1229-45.

[6] Mira Crouch and Heather McKenzie, The Logic of Small Samples in Interview-Based Qualitative Research, Social Science Information, December 2006, 45: 483-499.

Background reading

Whilst I was researching and writing this book, I found
a number of books on the topics of ageing and/or women
interesting. Here are some of them:

Athill, Diana *Somewhere Towards the End* (Granta, 2008)

De Hennezel, Marie *The Warmth of Your Heart Prevents Your
Body From Rusting* (Pan, 2012)

Ephron, Nora *I Feel Bad About My Neck* (Black Swan, 2008)

Moran, Caitlin *How to be a Woman* (Ebury, 2012)

Osler, Mirabel *The Rain Tree* (Bloomsbury, 2012)

Pillener, Karl and Brody, J *30 Lessons for Living* (Plume, 2012)

Sackville-West, Vita *All Passion Spent* (Virago modern classics, 1991)

Shilling, Jane *The Stranger in the Mirror* (Vintage, 2012)

Vaillant, George *Ageing Well: Guideposts for a happier Life*
(Little, Brown and Company, 2003)

Woolf, Virginia *A Room of One's Own* (Penguin Modern Classics,
2002)

Some favourite books as recommended by the twenty women

Out of sheer curiosity, I asked the women what their favourite
or inspirational books are. This difficult question received
a wide range of answers, sometimes reflecting their current
reading and sometimes pointing to books that they returned to
over the years. Here they are.

Anne	*Bess of Hardwick* by Mary S Lovell
	Hard Change by Dawn Reeves
Cecelia	*You Can Heal Your Life* by Louise L. Hay
	The Hidden Messages in Water by Dr Masaru

	The Shell Seekers by Rosamund Pilcher
Christine	*To Kill a Mockingbird* by Harper Lee
Helen	*A Book of Silence* by Sara Maitland
	The Secret Life of the Grown-up Brain by Barbara Strauch
Jane	*Flowers for Algenon* by Daniel Keyes
	Mister Pip by Lloyd Jones
	Crooked Letter Crooked Letter by Tom Franklin
Jeannie	Anton Chekov plays, and *What Katy Did* by Susan Coolidge
Kate	*The Shipping News* by Annie Proulx
Kitty	*Pride and Prejudice* by Jane Austen
Lesley	*The Poisonwood Bible* by Barbara Kingsolver
Liberty	*Troubles* by JG Farrell
Linda	*The Rainbow* by DH Lawrence
Madeline	*The Bible*
Margaret	*Frenchman's Creek* by Daphne du Maurier
	All Passion Spent by Vita Sackville-West
Marie	*Birdsong* by Sebastian Faulks
Nicole	*War and Peace* by Tolstoy
	Cutting for Stone by Abraham Verghese
Pat	*The Poisonwood Bible* by Barbara Kingsolver
Rose	*The Pursuit of Love* by Nancy Mitford
Simran	*Be Your Own Best Friend* by Mildred Newman and Bernard Berkowitz
Tanje	*Animal Farm* by George Orwell
Val	*Out of Our Minds* by Sir Ken Robinson
And me?	*I Capture the Castle* by Dodie Smith
	To Kill a Mockingbird by Harper Lee
	High Tide in Tucson by Barbara Kingsolver

ACKNOWLEDGEMENTS

A book cannot exist without a serious amount of support and input from other people. Many many thanks to my editor, Lisa; designer, Kate; and volunteer proof-readers, Bob, John and Ingrid. My wide ranging and valued group of cheer-leaders and critical readers include Pam, Julie, Dawn, Sarah M, Victoria, Jeanne, Claire, Sharron, Jane, Sarah G, Jude, Amanda, my brother and my parents. Without their encouragement, I would have given up a long time ago.

My family's patience, forbearance and continuing belief in me has been amazing, especially given some less than 'super mum' moments.

And, finally, my heartfelt thanks to the twenty women who took part. Their enthusiasm, candid reflection, trust, feedback and encouragement are what it's all about.

If you have enjoyed this book, you might like to leave a review on Amazon or Goodreads, and I would very much appreciate that.

I write a fortnightly newsletter too, if you would like to keep in touch. Sign up on **www.creatingfocus.org**.

With best wishes,

Sarah Dale

Twitter:
@creatingfocus

Facebook:
Sarah Dale – author

Lightning Source UK Ltd.
Milton Keynes UK
UKOW04f0621240114

225146UK00003B/18/P